letters from my incarcerated pen pals
sincerely, your friend

Bailey McManus

Copyright © 2025 by Bailey McManus
All rights reserved.

While the names and certain identifying details in this book have been changed to protect the privacy of individuals, the events described are based on actual occurrences.

No part of this publication may be reproduced in whole or in part, or stored in a retrieval system, or transmitted in any form or by any means, electronic, mechanical, photocopying, recording, or otherwise, without written permission of the author, except for the inclusion of brief quotations in a review.
For information regarding permission, please write to:
info@barringerpublishing.com

Barringer Publishing, Naples, Florida
www.barringerpublishing.com

Design and Layout by Linda S. Duider

Cover Photo by Alejandro Ruiz-Velasco Niembro

ISBN: 978-1-954396-79-1
Library of Congress Cataloging-in-Publication Data
Sincerely, Your Friend: Letters From My Incarcerated Pen Pals
by Bailey McManus

Printed in U.S.A.

For my pen pals

CONTENTS

How It Started................................. 1

Childhood Trauma 19

Juvenescence 46

Fatherlessness................................ 82

Drugs.. 105

Sentencing 124

Prison Life 149

After Prison 213

Friend Not Foe 245

After The Fact............................... 264

Drawings.................................... 269

Note from the author:
These letters have had sections removed for brevity and because pieces of our letters would not make sense without context. However, everything included is verbatim. I did not change what my pen pals wrote about their lives. All the following stories are true.

SINCERELY, YOUR FRIEND

Each of us is more than the worst thing we've ever done.

—Bryan Stevenson

YOU STILL *by Abraham Johnson*

Lost for words in the form of emotions
Told in tales of broken verbs
I've come unheard
I've come as a man with a plan that can withstand
The biggest damage done by the biggest evil
In the form of the biggest hand
Yet you still don't understand
Yet you still lack the compassion
To be compassionate for the less fortunate
For those children black white purple and red
With no shelter and who starve to death
Because they ate their last piece of bread
Yet you still lack the unconditional love
For that man, woman, and teenage child locked in
   a cell
Because maybe just maybe he or she followed
The only footsteps that they could comprehend
And helped them to come out of their shell
Lost in they own world with many stories to tell
But who will tell of their deepest secrets
And who will leak it so they opt to just not speak it
You still

HOW IT STARTED

Over the last eight years, I have connected with over 200 men in prison. *Sincerely, Your Friend* is a collection of letters and a window into the hearts and lives of American men in prisons across the country. These letters are combined with my research, providing a brief study of our nation's justice system and what we can do to decrease recidivism.

My pen pals wrote to me while in the midst of despair, suffering, shocking gratitude, and great hope. You have a chance to read what a few men wrote in their quiet moments to some girl they called a friend and see that these "criminals" are so much more than any crime.

I have done terrible things. I live with a lot of shame and guilt. But I did not go to prison for the crimes I committed because I am white, and I am a girl. That is the sad truth. People often didn't suspect me, and when they did, even when they knew for certain that I had done something against the law, they didn't care enough to do anything about it. The reality is I got a "get out of jail free" card when so many others did not. My criminal activity happened mostly during high school, but even as an adult, I have done things that I knew were wrong and hurt people I love.

In my experience, it is much easier to be a victim than to hurt other people. When I have made mistakes that hurt people, a part of me became convinced I was inherently evil. For people in prison, this belief is constantly reinforced. And as society reinforces these beliefs, we condemn people to a life of crime. In our fear and judgment, we become responsible. I do not know one person who hasn't been in the wrong sometimes, who hasn't inflicted pain. We are human, after all. And that's what this book is about. It's about our collective humanity and how it can be found *everywhere*, even in places no one expects to find it.

Writing people in prison happened by accident. I sent a request and a prayer by way of the U.S. Postal Service and found that for both me and the 180 people who responded, the request had been heard, the prayer answered.

I started writing people in prison when I was so sick I thought I might never have a normal life. Since kindergarten, I have undergone dull and sometimes debilitating headaches nearly every day, but as an adult, migraines were a constant. A choking, gasping feeling required an inhaler, though I did not have asthma. Simply walking across my living room could cause my pulse to race as if I had just run a mile. I collapsed onto the couch often, my heart pounding throughout my body. Ear infections came every two weeks as if fixed in my calendar. When I awoke at night, I stood to get out of bed and fell flat on the floor. I had grown accustomed to crawling. My arms and legs hurt so bad that I jumped and recoiled at the brush of a hand. I had a constant cold and was prone to angry, exhausted outbursts. I was only 21 years old.

It took almost a year of aggressive illness to uncover a diagnosis, which I was grateful to receive at all: Lyme disease. A common, rapidly growing illness in which doctors were mostly unaware of the severity and hesitant to treat. The antibiotics prescribed for Lyme Disease help most during the acute stages, but I suspected I had been living with Lyme disease for most of my life. The onset of more severe symptoms came after a concussion I got shortly after my twenty-first birthday.

Every morning, I awoke restless at 1:00 a.m., rose into the familiar darkness, and entered my quiet house. Nightmares plagued these nights and most every night of my life, but even in peaceful moments, I found I could not go back to sleep. Sometimes, I sat next to my precious son's bed and watched him sleep. Often, I slipped back into my own bed at five or six in the morning when the sun's rays had just begun to illuminate the rooftops and searched for a couple hours of sleep before my toddler awoke, asking for breakfast.

One insomniatic night, I tried as I always did to keep my eyes closed, to force myself to sleep. But my thoughts raced, and I found myself gazing again at the splashes of light painted across our ceiling. I was fed up with being sick all the time, fed up with putting all my energy into an unmoving, unchanging problem. I decided to create my own version of hope. If my life, for now, was to be dominated by illness, I would use these sleepless nights to make a difference—to do something meaningful.

Probably, the last thing I expected to do was lie in bed and think about world problems, but I had spent so much time staring at the ceiling, I had no choice but to let my mind loose to do as it pleases. Making videos on current world problems like climate change or transgenerational trauma passed through my thoughts. I considered spending my nights packing donation kits for homeless people. I also considered getting a second job, using this time to make a little extra money for my son and I to live a better life. But that required *committing* to nightly consciousness and somehow, my mind landed and got stuck on rehabilitation in American prisons. With this topic, for the first time since becoming desperately ill, my thoughts did not drain my energy but fueled it. I was excited.

People around the country are stuck in a cell all day, isolated and lacking means of expression. I wondered what I would need if I were them. My first thought was a friend, so I decided to be a pen pal. I think to some people this may seem drastic or far-fetched, but for me, it was simple. I have never been afraid of responsibility, am quick to take action, and often follow my heart into unexpected places. I thought perhaps letters could offer a small glimmer of light into another person's world—and mine. I got on my computer and looked up "how to write to someone in prison." What I found was pen pal services with thousands of names listed. People in prison paid a fee of less than one dollar for most sites, but even a dollar can carry enormous weight for an incarcerated person. One of these sites is how I met Dominic. I saw his photo—curly hair, kind eyes. There was something about him I trusted.

Dominic is the kind of person who starts every interaction with a hug. He is the best listener and spends our time writing and talking on the phone asking questions about my life and my past. Dominic was incarcerated for armed robbery as a young man and has been in prison for over twenty years. As the laws change over the years, Dominic watches men who committed the same crime he did or worse come and go from this prison, now often sentenced to a much shorter time. He worries daily about his parents. His father is on hospice, and his mother, a woman in her seventies, is his caretaker. Dominic blames himself for not being there to help. He reads legal books and fights his case to get a shorter sentence, but it is hard to catch a break when you are labeled a criminal. He still battles his case. His dream is to get out of prison so he can help his mom and say goodbye to his Pops. With his friendship, his story, and the example of tenacity he set, Dominic has shone far more light into my world than I could have ever hoped to offer him.

It is not my personality to dabble, to go halfway. When I started writing Dominic, I learned about his struggles as a young man in the criminal justice system and knew I could not settle for writing letters to just one person. I thought, if I pushed past the fatigue, the brain fog, the insomnia, the pain, maybe I could contribute to the world like I dreamed of doing when I was a child watching Oprah after school and asking Santa Clause for world peace. In his story, there was something I needed to learn, though I did not yet know what that was. I wondered how his life would be different if he had grown up in an affluent neighborhood or had teachers who invested in his future. My intention became making a bigger project of correspondence and potentially learning something valuable from their experiences. I hoped to discover patterns concerning how young people end up on the right path, or the wrong one. Interviewing people in prison, I thought, could inform the direction of a self-development book for young people I had wanted to work on for some time. Awake at 1:00 a.m., I opened my laptop and jotted the questions I had for struggling teenagers whose mistakes led them to time, maybe even a lifetime, behind bars. Questions morphed into a written interview, but at this point, it stayed a dream.

Scribbling letters to Dominic all those nights on my living room floor inspired me to eventually write all the people I did, but if not for my girlfriend, I would never have had the energy or capacity to pursue our correspondence. Mara. She was tenacious, only a year older than me and the CEO of a thriving business in town. When we first met, she was living Harry Potter-style at the bottom of a stairwell for $200 per month. She worked for pennies to turn around the business her father invested in and make it profitable. Everyone in our town admired her. We began dating only a month prior to the onset of my illness, but her care and dedication to our relationship carried me through the difficulties of that first enervated year—a year I barely remember.

While the prospect of writing people in prison was exciting, it did not cure my illness. Sadness morphed into despair as the physical illness impaired my relationships and the pursuit of my dreams. The aching in my chest became desperate. I knew I was in trouble and that my suffering deeply affected the people around me. My mind played with a belief that my family would be better off without me.

My son, Oliver, was with his dad for the weekend. I stumbled into his bedroom in search of clarity, purpose. I laid in his bed and watched the walls spin. *What am I still doing here?* I thought. *Maybe, I should run away. Be a monk. Never have to burden Mara or Oliver again.* He did not deserve a miserable, mess of a mom like me. I looked around his room. Paintings of Winnie the Pooh, Piglet, and Tigger hung carefully above his bed.

Oliver was an introvert. He was only three years old, but his tendency toward introversion was clear from infancy. Several weeks before, we received a massive refrigerator box and turned it into a castle, cutting holes for windows and doors. When guests came over, Oliver got quiet and sat in my lap for reassurance before disappearing into his castle. Sometimes, we found him there, engrossed in an imaginary world where cars smashed into each other and giant stuffed animals trampled calm and unassuming cities. One afternoon, I sat in his room, too weak to stand. Watching the light settle on his possessions then, his toys, the stuffed animals he cuddled each night, I knew that a son needs his mother, even if she is a mess. This special boy, my son, needed me.

My girlfriend found me there, my body sprawled across the wooden toddler bed. She knelt on the floor next to me, and for the first time since my sickness began over a year prior, she begged me to heal, to take drastic measures, to find a way out of this. She wept, pleading with me. *We can't live like this anymore.* And in a way, I received what I lost sight of during my illness: perspective. This wasn't about me. My health, my life, all of it was about my family. The darkness that had shrouded my life seemed to dissipate that instant. I made a decision. I did not care how many doctors I saw that would not or could not help me. I was taking my illness, and my life, into my own hands.

That night, I started my own version of physical therapy: yoga. I turned on a 10-minute restorative yoga video, which was basically stretching. I could not do half of it and spent most of those ten minutes lying on the floor, dizzy and panting. But I had started, and I was determined to make this an evening ritual, no matter how hard it was for me.

So much went into my healing. I cared for my body with exercise, nutrition, rest, supplementation, and I read dozens of books on healing from this specific illness. It was the intention behind my actions that caused healing to begin, the constant attention toward health that drew me closer to it, and the symptoms of an illness that shattered my life miraculously began to dissipate. No longer did I have to crawl to the bathroom at night. My balance was not fully restored, but slowly, I gained control over my body. Now, the headaches and whole-body pain could be calmed with pain relievers. Most days, I was able to fight through discomfort and agony alike to care for my son, go to work, and finally get to know Mara. She was the woman who took care of me when I got sick and helped me turn my life around, but until this point, I had been too ill to put in the energy necessary for our relationship to deepen.

I continued to regain my health. I continued to write to Dominic. This idea to write more people and to use their stories to put together a self-help book for teenagers stirred in me. But I was still held up by illness and the healing of it. Making something more of my curiosities about the unrevealed challenges of people who ended up behind bars was a dream that continued to drive my health to improve. Little did I know, another obstacle my friends and I corresponding would soon arise.

Mara grew up in a thirteen-person household with her parents and ten siblings. As a family, they bred cattle, managed orchards, kept about a dozen greenhouses, ran a large health food distribution company, and maintained about 2,000 acres of dryland wheat. At eight years old, she was given the option to take on the family's household chores in lieu of manual labor. Overseeing these indoor chores meant cooking and cleaning up after everyone in their household plus the dozens of family members who lived and worked on the farm. The five-story home my girlfriend grew up in contained multiple living rooms, a library, a sewing room, and a school room where all the children were homeschooled. Vacuuming alone could be considered an all-day project. She learned to rush to get it done. Even at a young age, Mara pushed her body and her mind to perform.

But learning about her life showed me the dark side of growing up as a farm kid. She had a close family but, in many ways, their lifestyle cost the children their adolescence. Though I admired her, when I looked at the woman who sometimes stayed up all night working for a salary of $200/month when she first became a business owner, I saw the little girl begging for her parents' love and approval.

Developing a relationship with my girlfriend's large family pressured me to give my three-year-old son a sibling. I saw how a family like hers interacted, how they had each other to lean on. They had childhood stories that made the difficult times a bonding experience rather than a traumatic one. Days working so hard on the farm that their hands bled were some of their best memories because it brought them closer together. When a family member was injured, or their mother lost another baby, they surrounded each other. This was the life I wanted for my son. I did not want him to have a childhood like mine where everyone was too traumatized and too selfish to be there for one another. He was three years old, and I felt like I was running out of time to give him a sibling close in age. I was healing, and I was writing, which brought hope back into my life. It was time. I simultaneously prepared letters for hundreds of inmates, and Mara and I applied to be foster parents.

We got the call on January 25th as I was on my way to work. Not one, not two, but three foster children: ages one, two, and three. They needed to be moved immediately. The agency would give us ten minutes to decide before they started making other calls, most likely splitting up the siblings. I pulled over and called Mara.

"Should we do it?" I asked.

She was busy at work. I could hear her shuffling in the background. "I don't know. What do you think?" The buzz of chatting employees was in the background. A girl who dropped her heroin addiction during pregnancy. A cousin, an aunt, an artist. Work, for her, was a community and home she patched together for those who needed one. Now, we were faced with the choice of creating another one. Three children. That was more than we expected.

How can you know? How can a person know such a thing with certainty? We just surrender and surrender and surrender again.

I sat in my car, quiet, looking out at the river and listening to the hum of cars fly past me. I called the certifier back and told her we would take the kids.

Sometimes things become clearer with perspective, but sometimes things just are, and we might always be asking why we chose to do what we did. Taking in three foster children was a minefield we were grossly unprepared for, a responsibility we could not know the true consequences of accepting. It was grueling. But in every challenge, in every minefield we faced, Mara and I gave thanks for the three children who turned our household into a family.

I knew nothing about their background. only their names and ages. Those first few days, all three had the stomach flu and their hair was covered in full-grown lice, but the hardest part of taking in these kids was not cleaning up vomit or picking lice out of their hair for hours. Taking care of them only brought us closer together. The real challenge was trying to instill trust in three wild children who had never known love. They spent their lives without boundaries or structure or care. As I discovered more about them, the enormity of raising three children with an abusive past hit me. There were many, many days I doubted it was possible for them to heal. I carried the weight that, even with my love, these precious children could find themselves in the same situation as Dominic. One in four children who age out of foster care are arrested during their first year of adulthood. Trauma worms its way into all our lives, and though the festering wounds of childhood create great struggle, they also brought our family closer together. My girlfriend, my children, Dominic—I understood them, and they understood me.

I had to find a way in the small moments that carried us through each day to laugh and be grateful for how our lives were changing. For children who screamed and cried for the entirety of every car ride, for finding my oldest daughter in the hallway and putting her back to bed 25 times each night before she finally felt safe enough to fall asleep, for asking my son to use nice words too many times to count, for learning how to deal with the abuse and anger that manifested in biting, hitting, scratching, hair pulling, tears, dirty faces, dirty butts, peed pants, poop on the wall, and 2:00 a.m. vomit. I was falling in love with these kids who froze in terror when they needed a diaper change and had nightmare after nightmare; kids who had already bounced around several foster homes. There were days I forgot to eat, nearly lost my children at the park, and days when I hid in the bathroom because all I could do was cry. I was grateful for all the challenging times because those were the times my kids pushed me to be a better human and the times that made us a family. Being a mom is not only watching your kids sleep at night and first steps. There are dance parties, putting underwear on your head, and chasing your kids around the house like a silly monster. But being a mom for me also became sitting on the floor while they scream, "I hate you! I hate you, you stupid Mommy," and trying to figure out what to do next.

On the night I first folded letters to a hundred men in cages across the country, the kids were asleep, the house quiet. Mara folded a massive pile of laundry on our green, shag carpet. We sat next to each other on the ground, the muted TV flashing pictures in our peripheral vision. The dishes that held our family meal were washed, and the house was quiet save the dull hum of a bedroom fan. We covered the floor with our projects and began folding. She took up most of the living room folding droves of tiny pants, socks, shirts, and jammies. I blanketed my corner of the carpet with papers and created a system for folding, writing addresses, and perfectly placing an American flag forever stamp in the top, right corner. These were monotonous tasks. But there was satisfaction as well. For her, the week's laundry was complete. For me, a new venture started.

I chose the recipients at random. I did not take the time to read their profiles. I did not look at their names or the state where they resided or even the reasons they ended up behind bars. It was April 2017. I was a 22-year-old woman about to send out hundreds of letters to men in prison. I remember chuckling to myself, remarking to my girlfriend that most people would think I was crazy. But as I prepared to mail the questions I had, I pushed away any fear that arose. Transparently, I did not think about stories I might hear or data I might gather in this wild, trial-by-error research quest of some young mom, a first-time writer. As I copied addresses from various pen pal websites off my hundred-dollar laptop covered in finger smudges, licked the envelopes until my tongue went dry, and cemented stamps to every corner, my heart raced for another reason. What if every one of these men hated me for writing them? I feared that, upon receiving the questions I had, they would respond with, "Who are you to ask me these things? You know I put my address online to meet friends, right? Not to answer questions from some unqualified researcher who has never even published a book." I hoped they would not resent me or despise me.

With each stamp placed on the letters that night, I placed down my hope that interviewing men in prison could turn into something real and meaningful. Maybe then, I could stop trying so hard. I was fighting for my worth. My world after college had become a prison. I wondered if this was how my pen pals felt. Even before prison, they felt locked up. If fighting for a purpose made them feel free too.

Despite the progress I had made with my health and family, I felt trapped in my body, trapped in the small town where I grew up, trapped in poverty, trapped even with these children I dearly loved. I had no money, no family who could help me. I did not know what to do but tried, day by day, to create some significance outside of motherhood. I strived to accomplish something great. Maybe then, I would not feel ashamed of myself. Maybe I could finally feel free.

My fear around writing to people in prison dissolved upon the arrival of those first letters. Stories not just of high school dropouts and police-crashed parties but of real pain and extraordinary grace. I could not believe it. These men did not hate me. Not only did they answer my questions, they shared their life story with me. What they said restored the meaning I lost in illness and trauma.

When I became pregnant with my son as an alcoholic teenager, I quit drinking because I had something outside of myself to fight for. Someone who needed me. Hearing these stories of people who were abused and who needed someone to confide in gave me a cause, something to serve outside of myself. Fighting for my health and my life was driven by my relationships: with Mara, my children, and now, my pen pals. Every day, I sat in a pink folding chair next to our mailbox and carefully read beautiful, tragic, heartbreaking stories. With each letter, my heart seemed to open up.

I wrote back—and wrote back and wrote back. I wrote until, like Mara's family on the farm, my wrists grew tired and creeping pain arose in my arms and hands. Yes, I worked like a farmer on those letters. It was an unfolding of the soul. It's funny how excitement heals. I was so excited to hear these stories, to respond, and to develop a friendship with these men. I wrote back to ask questions and explore what life is like in prison but also to acknowledge them for coming out the other end of lifelong trauma with gratitude and perspective. Dominic was the only pen pal I planned to write continuously, but once I read these letters, I couldn't help but stay in touch with everyone who responded.

In that first letter, I typed a short series of questions about their high school experiences and their lives growing up. I asked about school. What I got were stories of trauma. Trauma leaking into people's lives, pooling around things most important to them: their families, their health, their freedom. They shared with me what I would have never thought to ask. They shared their hearts. From the darkest, loneliest, most isolated place came light. I found more and more of it every day as I opened my mailbox to find it jam-packed with eager letters.

But as an increasing number of letters arrived, I realized I was not going to be as good of a friend as I had hoped. Sometimes I received dozens of letters in a single week, requiring me to write twenty letters every other day just to keep up. And I was not able to keep up. Sometimes, it took me months to respond. I asked my pen pals' forgiveness and signed each letter "Sincerely, Your Friend." I shared with complete sincerity that our letters had fostered a friendship I desperately needed. Being a parent is a lonely occupation, a loneliness made worse by illness. Getting to know my pen pals filled that void for human connection I was missing.

It might sound odd, but when I first started writing my pen pals, I felt self-conscious that I had no number after my name. I never wanted to make them feel like they were defined by the number assigned to them or by their current situation. For me, these letters dismantled the stigma around a prison sentence because, by getting to know them, any previous fear of people in prison was extinguished.

Prior to our correspondence, I felt like a failure. Being extremely ill, I backed out of my collegiate pursuits to focus on health and family. Dropping out of my bachelor's program felt like abandoning my dreams. Community college had been a time of great success for me. I started school at nineteen with a two-month-old baby while living off a $350/month welfare check. Upon starting school, state assistance was about to run out.

We were staying at my father's house then, in my old room where I lived off and on throughout childhood. My memories mostly include his face in mine, being screamed at for spilling water, sneaking a spoonful of sugar, or taking too long to brush my teeth. Every morning after my son was born, I woke up like I always had in those times I lived with my father—to yelling and cussing in the back room, a bang or crash against the washer or coffee pot. Maybe it was the rinse cycle that set him off or the coffee timer or a phone call or the television. He did not do well with interactions of any kind. Mostly, he sat on the couch watching surfing documentaries or *The Simpsons*. I left him alone. I stayed in my bedroom, stayed to myself, wishing my mother was more stable so I could live with her.

I begged the parents of a childhood friend to let my son and I live in their guest house. With mercy for my desperation, they agreed and charged me $200/month. I had $150 left for gas, diapers, and groceries. I got a job at a local fish market, and my new baby, only two months old, started going to daycare so I could go to school and find a way to a better life.

There was hope. In my first term at community college, I saw a flier for Phi Theta Kappa, an honor society. In that moment, my childhood dream of going to a great school, becoming a doctor, and saving children around the world flooded back to me. Suddenly it became clear. This was how I would take care of my family and save myself from an optionless life.

Because I had a new baby, I took classes only two days a week. They were 10-hour days, and I had to sit on the floor of a bathroom stall between classes to pump. But I was doing it. I sat next to the toilet, inhaled a sandwich, closed my eyes, and laid my head back while I chewed, exhausted. Oliver spent half the night awake as a baby, so I spent three quarters of the night awake to get my homework done. The school was small, and the bathrooms were not very busy, but when someone did come in, my eyes shot open. I made myself very quiet, pausing mid-chew. The only sound was the slow whir of the breast pump the health department gave me. My face turned red, and I felt hot. I was ashamed to be pumping in the bathroom, to be eating on the floor, and to be in college. I was ashamed to be myself at all. Every interaction was cause for anxiety. Being constantly belittled at home and throughout childhood, it felt like I had to be invisible. I held a belief that any misspoken word could cause people to not just be bothered by me but to hate my guts. Everyone I met in school seemed to have their life more figured out than I did.

I found out in those first few months of college that I, Bailey McManus, was actually smart. This came as a shock. I never had any opportunity prior to college to learn about myself in this way. Over and over again, I have found that my pen pals experienced the same thing I did. Most of the people I have written did not have someone to pay for or take them to soccer practice, piano lessons, camps, or church groups. We did not have people pushing us to take AP classes or help us with our homework after school. But I got a chance to learn about myself in college, a chance I wish every one of my pen pals could receive. I know that, if they had an opportunity for education, they would blossom and thrive just as I did.

Dropping out of school when I was very ill terrified me. When I began to receive these incredible letters, I reclaimed authentic parts of myself hidden in the shadow of my illness. These friendships gave me hope again. I thought maybe I could have it all. Perhaps, I could be an amazing mom, write a book, and have a meaningful life.

Everything I learned about struggle, and what I hoped to write about upon receiving responses from the initial letters I sent, was set on the back burner. The plan was to write a self-help book for teenagers, using data from interviews to inform the direction of that book. I actually interviewed many people other than my pen pals during this time. I have hours and hours of recorded interviews conducted in person and over the phone. However, it did not take long for me to see that this story, *their* story, was begging to be told. I wanted to write the book that I needed as a teenager, but I *needed* to write an ode, an homage to the people I knew were lost in a failing system. I witnessed the power in their stories. A powerful story demands to be told.

In the process of befriending people behind bars, I learned about how they are locked away and stigmatized for the rest of their lives for crimes that, to me, seemed unavoidable given their upbringing. Trauma was crippling to people in prison, and the system did more than lack care for my pen pals who were mostly young, minority men. The justice system pushed for their incarceration. Though I suspected from the beginning that there was more to prisoners than the stereotype placed upon them, I was still letting go of the classic idea most people have of people who commit crimes in America. I did not expect to hear from people who were reading philosophy from their cots in solitary confinement or dreaming of building businesses and creating a stable family life for their kids.

What I heard about prison prior to this correspondence mostly came from my boss. Every day, I went to work at a local Native American fish market. The days were slow and relaxed. My boss, Richard, was a kind man, a veteran who grew up on a reservation in Eastern Washington and served as a firefighter in the Navy. Rich was tall, quiet, and kind. He let people be themselves around him. Rich walked with a limp because of a car accident that happened when he was a teenager. That accident ruined his basketball career and killed his cousin who was also his teammate and best friend. Despite severe injuries, he continued to play basketball, traveling the country with a club team, playing in churches and high schools with other reservation kids desperate for a game. But after a tournament, when everyone else was partying, Rich stayed in the hotel room. He preferred to watch TV or sit at a quiet dinner table with a small group of friends. Rich talks about how while his friends were out cheating on their wives, he brought the elder women flowers. I once overheard Rich mention his incarceration to a friend and wondered what this man could have done to end up in prison.

His mother was a social worker and provided opportunities for connection and growth on their reservation in a way no one else had. His father was the warden at the juvenile detention center, so every cop in town knew Rich. If he got into trouble, there was no way to hide it from his parents whom he respected immensely. During Rich's upbringing, his parents housed hundreds of foster children. Some were brought to them through the state. Others came and went when they had no food, housing, parents, or money. Rich said he woke up every day to a house full of kids who were often not there the night before. He would come down from his room and start pouring bowls of cereal for his schoolmates who crowded the kitchen counter while others lay asleep on the floor and couch. The example his parents set taught him to be a man, and he was a good one.

Rich treated his employees with the utmost kindness and respect. He encouraged us during lapses in customers to do our homework, read a book, or just sit back and listen to the reggae music that blared from our SiriusXM radio. It was a safe place for me. I filleted massive, wild-caught salmon dip-netted by Native anglers from a wooden platform above the waterfalls of the Klickitat River. They fished at night, which was dangerous. Every tribe lost a few people each year to this way of traditional fishing, but it was hard for the young men to resist. It was both lucrative and brought them closer to their history as Native Americans. The young fishermen I knew sent most of their money to families back home, buying toys for their nieces and nephews, flowers for their sisters, mothers, and grandmothers, and food for the whole family. Most of the young fishermen we worked with were not close to their fathers. The men leading crews often treated their fishermen like sons. They camped together on the rocks. They fought through the night together for a fish, each morning coming together at an elder's house for breakfast. Every week, they would sweat at the longhouse together. They sat with elders who discussed happenings in the tribe and shared everything they knew.

Working for Richard made me proud. I wanted to sell as much salmon as I could. Not only did he treat his employees well, but every dollar we made for him was given back to the Native community tenfold. By increasing the demand for salmon, we increased the economic prosperity of surrounding Native American communities.

Rich was a born businessman. He started businesses during his time in prison and had been working on the idea for a fish market throughout his sentence. He started the fish stand the day of his release. He bought a truck, made a sign from a piece of plywood, got a few fish and a cooler, and started selling fish on the side of the road.

A year into our friendship, he told me the story of his arrest.

After that horrific car accident when he was a teenager, his hip was destroyed, and he struggled with crippling pain. He started smoking weed, which back then was illegal and harshly punished. He said it helped him, so he continued, and he started selling to his friends. Because it was hard to acquire, he was making trips down south to pick up bulk, vacuum-sealed bags of California weed. He hung a feather in his rearview mirror for luck and prayed for the best.

On the day it happened, he said he knew it was coming. A young man begged to come with him. He needed a ride north close to where my boss was headed. This man, Rich told me, was black. Rich was not prejudiced, but he didn't miss a thing. He knew how racist the criminal justice system was. He told me, "I'm a half-breed. My father is a white warden. I know how to talk to a cop. I'll be just fine by myself. But you get a black dude in the car, there's nothing I can do to smooth talk. That car's getting searched." And, that's exactly what happened. Rich had done that drive dozens of times with no trouble, but on that day, the two of them were arrested and sent to prison. Rich had to call his parents from jail to disappoint them and his three younger siblings with the news of his arrest.

I was proud to be his friend, so if Rich told customers about his prison sentence, and I saw a glimmer of judgment in their eyes, I stood tall, letting them know it did not matter what this man had done. I want to think my faith contributed to the faith other people had in him, but that would not be true. Rich did not need help gaining trust. He was a good man through and through. Anyone could see that. People were drawn to him because he did not need anyone to be anything but themselves. He was your friend. He lived a simple life and was content. In my experience, he always did right by people. He was a hero, in a way, to all of us in the community. He was an actual hero too, a veteran firefighter for the Navy. It's not for me to say whether he deserved his prison sentence, but he certainly did not deserve judgment for it. It got me thinking that people who go to prison are just people. After knowing Rich, I cannot believe a prison sentence says much about a person's character.

Rich always seemed to pull up in his big, blue truck covered in fish guts during the times I was responding to letters. I kept the stacks of letters in a blue binder that also held blank paper and poems and articles I printed to share with my pen pals. Hesitantly and after some questioning, I shared with him what I was doing—writing pen pals in prison, a couple hundred of them.

I feared the resistance I knew I would encounter. The perception he had of prisoners was different from mine. He experienced the hard parts: fights, pettiness, drugs, the victim mentality. But I had seen all of those behaviors in the teenagers I went to high school with and the alcoholic adults I grew up around. I could see past the hard parts and know that these people were more than the bad things they had done. Rich wanted to protect me, but I was committed to these relationships. In their letters, I saw their hearts. I knew what it felt like to be abandoned and to be so crippled by trauma that making the right decisions did not feel possible. I encountered resistance from Rich and many others, but I refused to be another person who gave up on my new friends.

On top of my new respect for people behind bars and the friendships I was developing behind bars, research I began to do about incarceration in America led me to exactly what I expected—an ill-equipped system, crippled under the weight of bias and two million prisoners. The people it fails are almost always underprivileged. It is almost never the wealthy, white people who end up in prison. Mostly, incarcerated people in America are born into poverty, neglect, abuse, and a racist society. Blacks are six times more likely to go to prison than whites. Offenders are 13 times more likely to have grown up with significant childhood trauma. One in 25 people on death row are falsely convicted. One in five African Americans in prison are serving a life sentence. Research on American prisons has proven that these rates are not because people from minority demographics commit more crime. These statistics represent a system that is not fair and is not helpful. People are not often transformed into productive members of society during their incarceration. Many are released even more traumatized and with fewer opportunities to change the trajectory of their lives.

Belonging in this world is a basic truth. Corresponding with my pen pals helped me open my heart to the inherent belonging we all share. I believe every person deserves to experience their belonging in the world. It was easy to include inmates in this belief and much harder to include myself. But befriending people who had robbed and even murdered other human beings forced me to look at myself and consider that I might be worthy of experiencing happiness in this world, of belonging in it. My family and these letters gave me a level of purpose and meaning I never foresaw. This meaning outshone any goal or accomplishment. It was bigger than me. Relationship heals.

I needed letters from these prisoners as much as they needed letters from me. My pen pals sent me my only Christmas cards and encouraged me on my path more than any friend or family member. They shared their honest hopes and deepest desires with me. I came to earnestly believe that people are much more than the crimes they have committed. Oscar Wilde observed that, "the truth is rarely pure and never simple," which is certainly the truth of incarceration. The friends I made these last seven years are more than a crime or a prison sentence. Getting to know them propelled me into my own life. Their stories and struggles drove me to write but also to get out of bed, to work, to care for my children. These men, my friends, inspired me to live.

CHILDHOOD TRAUMA

I once heard a story that taught me everything I need to know about solving recidivism and mass incarceration. In the story, when a tribal woman finds out she is pregnant, she goes into the wilderness with the people she is closest to and searches her soul, listening for a song. When the notes find her, floating from the heavens or crashing upon her like waves, she and her loved ones memorize it, return to the tribe, and teach every villager how to sing the melody of this new baby. Upon the child's arrival, the song is sung to him or her for the first time. And on meaningful and momentous occasions in this child's life, the tribe comes together to sing this special human their unique melody. They hear the song on their wedding day, in triumphs, and, eventually, it will be sung to mourn their death.

In their song, the villager is consistently reminded of who he or she is. And if this villager happens to lose their way, the entire village comes together. When a crime or betrayal occurs, the townspeople recognize this person has forgotten who they are. A circle gathers, placing the wandering soul between everyone who loves and knows them. Then, they sing. They all sing the person back to their true self.[1]

I cannot tell you how many times I have wished for a song and wished for a community to sing it to me. I have had countless moments where I felt hopeless and desperate and lost. I have needed to be reminded that I am loved and that I am not alone. The men I've written have not necessarily been at the most lost point in their lives when we met. That came before incarceration. In fact, I think the people I have written experienced more clarity around the time we wrote each other than they ever have because the nature of imprisonment forces people into such isolation that they have to face their hardships and truths. However, to rob, to kill, to rape, to vandalize, to abuse and sell drugs, a person must be quite lost. Criminality does not make a person inherently bad. It makes them lost. When a person commits a crime in the United States, we tell them they are not worthy of a song. We strip them of everything they are, lock them away, and tell them they are evil and useless. We need some kind of guide, a way to rehabilitate and bring them back to their truth—that they are worthy of a song. That they are here, in this world, because they belong.

The beginning of criminal activity does not actually start with crime. To understand why a crime was committed, we have to go back to the beginning and examine a person's young life. With most people in prison, I believe we would find that the sounds of their world were too brash and discordant for a song to be heard.

There is a strong link between trauma and violent and reckless behavior because of how trauma affects our brains. Some studies have even shown people who commit crimes to be 13 times more likely to have ACES.[2] The well-developed and researched ACES (Adverse Childhood Experiences) Test asks questions about childhood trauma and has been shown to predict a lot about a person's future by analyzing their past. There are preventative measures that can be taken such as therapy, education, and rehabilitative programs during and after prison. We now know anger and impulsiveness can be detected in a brain scan and even cured. Amen Clinics has proven this after 200,000 brain scans.[3] A person's future is not set in stone. It is created, and it can be shifted.

When we experience moments of fear, our ability to think and reason dissipates. Our IQ goes down tremendously—up to 40 points! Our prefrontal cortex is no longer in charge, and the primal parts of our brain kick in to help us survive.[4] I have personally experienced how being in fight or flight can turn off a brains' ability to think.

Both of my parents were horribly abused as children, especially my mother. Their fears for my life were pervasive throughout my childhood. I was often warned about sexual predators and kidnappers. They told me, if someone tries to steal you, scream. I used to practice screaming so I would be ready if that day ever came, and I was convinced it would. My worst fear as a child was the inability to scream. That I might be in a situation where my voice gave out. When I was 16 years old, my worst fear came true. My boyfriend, whom I had just broken up with for cheating, found me at a house party, grabbed me by the hood of my sweatshirt, and threw me down a flight of stairs. I fell backward and slammed into a wall. He took my hood again so quickly I didn't have time to react and dragged me down another flight, the hood of my sweatshirt pulling against my neck and choking me. Even after he had let go, I remember losing the ability to think, to cry, or to scream. My worst fear came true. I could only crawl up the stairs and stumble into a group of friends for help. Situations like these, stacked on top of each other, depleted my ability to reason for a long time.

In the letters I received, my pen pals shared their life stories with me—tragic, heartbreaking, beautiful, lonely, and meaningful stories. It changed my life in an unexplainable way to open my mailbox and pull out the life stories of men like this. Men locked away who held much deeper cages within them. And I saw, as if in a reflection, how trauma can shape decisions we make and the course of our lives.

AVERAGE URBAN KID'S LIFE

Bailey,

Yes, I'm in a cell by myself all day long except for one hour a day. I get recreation in a dayroom area which is a cage with bars surrounded by the cells so everybody is either looking at you or talking to you, kind of feel like an animal at the zoo. I usually pass my time by either working out, drawing or reading. I have a couple of books that I've picked up here and there. I use to have my sister send me books or my mother but my sister passed away about a yr ½ ago and my mother is now in a hospice center so I do what I can to get what is needed. My life was the average urban kid's life . . . My mother broke her back when I was like 8. She was drunk and fell off the balcony. She later learned how to walk so she continue to raise 3 boys and a girl. My father was always in and out of prison. When he was home he used my mother as a punching bag. My oldest brother was slow, and my middle brother later died at 14 from AIDS which turn my mother into a full blown alcoholic then one day my father is beating my mother. My brother wakes me up to tell me and next thing you know him and I are fighting. By this time I had already started gang banging so long story short I shot him in the shoulder. He left and he's never hit my mother since. I raised my sister and older brother while my mother drank her life away. I love her though. Hate her for being an alcoholic, but love her for still being my mother and not giving up on us after my brother died. I later got a girl pregnant at 14 and had my son at 15 and have been living on my own since. Later on in life my stories are mostly based on incarceration. Thanks for writing and hope to hear from you again soon.

Wyatt Hernandez

MENTALLY I'M SHUTTING DOWN

Hi Bailey,

I was taken away from my birth parents at three and adopted at the age of five. At seven my adopted parents told me my birth mom died. She was only thirty-three. So that did a lot of damage to me. I also saw a lot of domestic violence as a young child from birth to three. I remember too much at such a young age! So I had a lot of issues as a kid. When I was 12, I tried to kill myself. I was very close, so I got sent to a mental hospital. I've been in and out of mental hospitals and group homes from 12-16. Then, I got in legal trouble at 18, and I've been in and out of jail until I caught a prison bid. I've been locked down in a 8 by 4 ft room for the past 2 months, so mentally I'm shutting down. I'm going through a rough patch right now. I am really depressed. But this nice person named Bailey has brought some light into this black cave.

Sincerely your pen pal,
Mike O.

I'VE BEEN RUNNING

Dear Bailey,

Hey! I am very thankful for you considering replying back to my letter. I wanted to help you with your research due to the fact I thought to myself if I had help when I was a kid, I wouldn't be here now serving a 5-year sentence. But everyone has a life story so here's mine.

I was born in a small town in east Texas, but at 8 months old, I moved with my mother to her hometown in Louisiana. I stayed there with her until I was 14. Living with my mom and my older sister, we went through hard times like a lot of other single parents go through from lights and water cut off to not having enough food to eat for the three of us, but we always pull through together. On April 23, 2004, my life changed forever. At 2:00am, I woke up hearing someone screaming to the top of their lungs. I jumped off my top bunk and ran towards the screaming, which was coming from my mother and stepfather's bedroom. When I got there, what I saw still is unbelievable to my eyes to this day. My older sister was screaming, pulling my mom's arm saying, "Why!" That's when I noticed she had a small hole in her chest near her heart. She shot herself while my stepdad was asleep beside. After that I was forced to move in with my Dad. We had a good relationship. But after that, I felt abandoned. I felt lost. None of it made any sense, and at the age of 14, I wanted answers that no one could give me. My heart was broken because the one person I loved the most and who was always there when I didn't know what to do was gone forever. I thought about and tried similar ways to go out like she did in order to escape reality. My father is a very good dad no doubt, but that was my problem. He was my dad, not my mom. So to take away reality, I started smoking weed and drinking, and after that it went to cocaine and X pills. Drugs took my pain away. At times, I would get so high and cry and scream. I hated her for leaving me like she did. In the midst of doing drugs, I dropped out of school and ran the streets, stealing and robbing in order to get high and escape reality once again. And that's why I'm here now. I've been running from my reality my whole life. Now, I've been forced to face it, and so I have. I have defeated it. It's sad to say but it's the truth. Coming to prison was good for me because I overcame my fear and I realized the answer I wanted will never be answered. By my mother doing what she did, she put me in her shoes, so as I've sat in here over the years, I understand my mom was going through something. What, I don't know, but I do know I must not do the same because I have to be strong for her, my two sisters, and myself.

Hope to hear from you soon.

Respectfully,
Marques Jr.

WHAT I WASN'T PREPARED FOR

Bailey,

"What would life be like if we had no courage to attempt anything?" —Vincent Van Gogh

I received the post cards you sent. That was nice—Thanx! My sister, yeah, she was pretty cool . . . She was 31 when she passed away. Three children, single parent—all children by the same guy. Her and the father had been apart for like two years then she met this dude who later killed her. But she graduated high school, worked at the hospital, was funny, believed in family, sometimes shy, and would fight like hell to defend me from anyone that dared talk down on me.

You know Bailey, I'm from San Antonio and grew up on the streets, in and out of facilities. My mother was a drunk, but did the best she could for us. My father used to beat my mother until I was old enough to defend her and ended up doing all the fighting for her whenever he was around. Most times he was locked up himself. Then, I got involved with gangs, roaming the streets while still raising my sister. I said all that to say that I've been through hell and back, and not once have I blinked twice knowing the life I lived has many downs but accepted. What I wasn't prepared for was my sister dying on me.

Sincerely,
Wyatt

MY DADDY

Dear Bailey,

Well . . . ain't this some shit on MLK Day I got into a fight. I wish the report told you how it started. Know this about me, I can't stand white people that try to act black. Just because one brotha lets his white friend say "nigga" doesn't mean other brothas is cool hearing it. I'm mad it happened 11 months out of the hole. Had a good job. Had people I was training. My blood brother just was doing the video visits with me. I was able to see my niece and nephew.

I love how you said, "I forget there's hope." I do too. Have you ever felt like life can't get worse? I'm in the hole a lot, but I hate it. I gotta battle my demons every time to make good choices.

Not all the time but sometimes, I will be real, the way I was raised by my birth family you would literally be like what the fuck. How could a dad tell his daughter, "You better stop runnin round at night and sleepin wit niggas for free." My dad tried telling me as a teen the most valuable thing about a woman is her pussy cause it's a gold mine. Every man wants pleasure. My daddy born and raised in Detroit in the late 70s. He told me not to steal then he has me waiting outside a dope house him and his brother tryna rob. Then I see him again when I'm 16 he tells me to bring him a gun, so I steal one from a car. He pulls off a robbery gets the stuff (some jewelry and $1600) and on the way out he gets shot in the shoulder by a 13-year-old boy. Mind you this is the second time he has been shot when I'm around. He starts shooting back, gives me the lot. I had to hide it. I ended up hiding it under the wheel well of a car on bricks. Long story short I took him to the hospital. I don't even know why I brought that up. My dad gets me on one. Even my dad wants peace and love.

His dad hung him by extension cords and beat on him till he passed out. His daddy was a guerilla pimp and had him watch as he beat on women. Then how was I born? My daddy had my mom hoeing. She was too good looking to let her waste it. She got pregnant and had me. I'mma end this before I rant.

It doesn't bother me how it takes you "forever" to write back. When you do write back it's much more meaningful. I'm not upset. I understand. Life's busy. Be smooth.

*Love,
Damien*

SPEAK UP

Every move I make brings me closer
With every breath I take it gets deeper.
Enough is never enough
My voice isn't being heard,
These walls are caving in
Yet you choose not to see it
What will it take for you to believe me?
Haven't my actions caused awareness to
My problems!
All these red flags
Hatred, abuse, addiction, self inflicted pain,
A melting of mental trauma
The fear of breaking this family apart
So I hold it in,
I can't lose you even though you hurt me
I love you,
I should have spoken up.
Maybe then my life wouldn't be so
Difficult. I've learned a lot in this game of life.
Empathy, courage, wisdom.
All of which I can bestow upon any who will
Listen.

Think before you act.

If something's wrong, ask for help.
Never hold it in. Speak up.

By Ian Wagner

THE NUMBER ONE THING

Bailey

First and foremost, I wanna thank you for taking the time to read my letter and writing me back. If I'm being honest, Joel let me read that last you sent him so I could get a better understanding and a little more of your story, so I'm also gonna go off of that, cool?

Well, yes writing has always been a big dream of mine and still is, but I feel like there's always something getting in the way; like all this prison bull-shit. I'm trapped, and my mind is as well. Does that make sense? Overall, that's my biggest goal. For now, I'm going to school to better myself: spelling, writing, and checking out books that can school my mind and teach me how to write.

Some of my plans and goals for the future . . . Well, Bailey, I'll be lying if I sit here and tell you I have it all figured out cuz I'm far from knowing. I mean, I became a man in this place, and I've never had my own place, car, or job. Before getting locked up at 15 years old, I had a hard life. Since I could remember my mom was always on drugs. Everyone always said after my second baby sister passed away she just lost it and gave up on life. My dad was never in this picture. Well, when he wanted he would come around. Out of these 11 years I've been in prison, I probably got one letter. So around 13 years old I was running the hood living with friends, homies, family members, and then I met my lady who I lived with until I got locked up at 15 years old. She was by my side through the whole five. That's what I did the first time I came down. I got out in 2012 for 2 months. When I was out I got her pregnant. We now have a baby boy. He's my Junior. That's my world and is a big reason why I'm trying to be a better man.

Before I got lost in all that, if I had to come up with an answer for my goals: 1. Keep studying and become a better writer. 2. Open a tattoo shop. Art is a big part of my life, and even though we're not supposed to tattoo in here, that's something I do to better my craft and make little side money. Let me know what kinda stuff you like, and I'll be more than happy to draw for you. Overall, I wanna help people and just put myself in a position where I can give back and be happy while doing it. Giving back is something I love and wanna do and feel like I have to do.

You also asked what I wish I knew when I was younger. That I didn't have to follow what everyone else was doing. I could go my own way and stay doing what I loved, and that was playing football—sports. And not to give in to drugs, something I believe we all somewhat been through by some way or another, and I feel like that's the number one thing that's a problem with kids and teens now. Like if they only knew what it takes away from family, friends, etc, they would probably think too, you feel me? I learned to hate drugs for the simple fact that it messed up my whole family, took away the people I love, and even to this very day is stopping my mom and family from being the people I wish and know they can be. But you wanna know something? I wouldn't change my past. I believe going through all of that made me who I am now, and I love me. Maybe I had to go through all of this in order to help and understand other people, kids, teens. I mean like yourself. You had a hard life and been down the dark road and understand how it feels to be at your lowest, and now you're at somewhat your highest and know it's only gonna get better.

Before I close, I just want you to know I'm very thankful for your time. I know life is hard, but just stop and take a good look around you. You're blessed. To have food and water and a place to lay your head is a good day. I'll close with hopes of hearing back from you soon.

Benjamin Guzman

FORGIVENESS

Dear Bailey,

Thank you for your letter of encouragement. It actually helped a lot, and your article about forgiveness took the weight of the world off my shoulders. Because I've been struggling with the death of my sister since 2016 when a drunk driver ran her over, and I haven't learned how to forgive, but that letter helped a lot. Even though he only got 10 years, I've learned to cope with it now. I also thank you for believing in me about my company. I can't wait. Maybe when I get out, my first grill will be made for you and your family, and I will ship it there. I'm glad the kids are good, and I hope it does snow for y'all so you can go sledding.

Wishing you well.
Gunner White

I NEED A GENUINE FRIEND

Dear Bailey,

My name is Ben Crawland. I am 23, grew up in a small town supported by the mill. My friend gave me your info because I recently had the worst moment of my life, a complete rock bottom. I was engaged to be married. That was great until she broke it off yesterday. So my friend said you're married, which is legit going to be the single first time I have spoken to a girl this much without flirting. I suffer from severe sex addiction, and I think it's because I was raped at age 18 by a guy and three women at a hotel. So if you think it's ok, I would like to write you once a week? Look, I need a genuine friend because I am struggling with self esteem. I feel unwanted and alone, so I need a normal person to person straight forward interaction. I look forward to hearing from you, Bailey. Whatever you feel comfortable with.

Ben Crawland

SENSITIVE TOWARDS LOVE

Hey Bailey,

What's going on? I hope this letter finds you in the best of health mentally, physically, emotionally, and spiritually. This is the letter I stated I would write to you about sharing my past with you. I'm kind of nervous. Ok, where do I start ummm . . . Well, when I was growing up I struggled a lot in school. It was hard for me to stay focused, and my attention span was very short. I used to have trouble with teachers, just about all my teachers, and I was diagnosed with ADHD at a very young age. I mean you couldn't give me sweets, you couldn't show something fun for the first time. I was just about you know what. They diagnosed me as a very hyperactive kid. And some of why I would have trouble at school is because I wasn't getting the nourishment and nurture and attention at home. And I'll never forget this. I came to school, I think I was in the like 2nd or 3rd grade, came into class with my head down, and I immediately sat and put my head on my desk, and you could just see my countenance. My teacher walked up to my desk and asked me, "What's wrong, Alec?" I said my mom went back to jail, and I was very grieved, and she told me "I figured that." I was like, are you serious? That's all you have to say?

    My grandmother raised me, and she did the best she could. She would verbally abuse me and physically abuse me, but that was her way of raising me in her eyes. I mean she wouldn't let me go outside and play besides going to the mailbox and checking the mail and taking the trash out. I'm not kidding you, it was hell to be honest. So she had this friend that she would trade pain medications with and muscle relaxers. Any time she would receive her prescription, she would send me to the friend's house to trade the medications with her friend.

So whatever her friend didn't have my grandmother had so they traded. So her friend had a granddaughter. And one day she called my grandmother and asked her if I could come over for something. My grandmother didn't think nothing of it so she let me go. Mind you, my grandmother and her friend lived in the same apartment complex. So I just had to walk to a different apartment building. I'm a kid, maybe 7 or 8 years old. I arrive there, and she took me to her back room where she molest me, and I mean she had me doing all kinds of things, very sexual horrible things that shouldnt be exposed to a 7-8 year old.

Her grandmother wasn't there the first time. There would be times where my grandmother would be at work, and she would watch me until my granny got off so after school I would just go to they house. Man, you know I'm thinking it's cool because Im old enough to know that this is sex, but I'm not thinking that this is a spiritual setup that's behind this or that this took root in my heart and can destroy me later. So this happen a few times. My mom is still locked up. My grandmother is raising me doing the best she can, and I have no father figure. Still to this day I don't know my father. I didn't experience the affirmation from my father. I didn't experience the affirmation from my father, nor my mother. So you talking about somebody lonely, degraded, sad, grieved, all these are understatements. So my mom gets out she back on this bullxxxx and I literally ran the streets with my mom at all times of the night. She would leave me at other folks house, I mean I literally saw my mom smoke crack rocks, prostitute— literally have sex for money. I mean you name it, she did it right in front of me.

My sister had left a long time ago, so it would be me and my mother rip and running the streets. My sister ran off to her dad's house so I'm just stuck with my mother. All through my mom's addiction to drugs and alcohol she would just up and leave, I mean literally. We would be out in the streets all times of the night, and we would go to my granny house. The next morning I would wake up, and she would be gone or in the middle of the night. She would drop me off at different people's houses and come back the next day. Little did I know this would cost me relationships with women.

Anytime I feel depressed, sad, or lonely, these feelings from my childhood resurface. I'm very sensitive towards love. It's like I automatically open up towards it. Especially if I'm giving a part of me to it whatever the object is. The same feeling I felt when my mother used to leave me when I was a kid comes back to my present more vividly. I feel like something is missing, so I try to find joy and happiness through materialistic things or other people. So I tend without even realizing it to cling to certain people or certain things not even aware that they cannot meet my desperate needs. I try to find security or love through people that don't understand my emotions. They may say they do, but in all actuality they don't. Why? Because they don't even understand they self. So they begin to use your emotions to their benefit and people use them to control others or take advantage of them. Some people shut and push others out. I feel rejected at times because when I was a kid that's all I felt—rejected and misused

So growing up all throughout my teens I knew love and security was something I needed. Without even realizing it I opened myself up to it. Being lonely was something I felt strongly because my mom left me. I wasn't aware that I was trying to fill a void with other things such as: pornography, money, drugs, women, and whatever else I felt like I could try to meet my needs with. Sweetie, to be honest only God can fill the void that we're desperately trying to fill.

I'll never forget this one Saturday. I went to a church function, and this lady called my name, and she began to prophesy over my life. A prophet is a person who literally speaks for God. God speaks through that person through the holy spirit. She began to tell me what I've been doing that was wrong that I thought I was doing right. She told me how I've been molested, and that's how lust began to take root in my heart. And how I would masturbate to fulfill these strong lustful desires of my flesh. And then she said if I continue to do what I do, I'll dig myself a hole that's so deep no one would be able to help me. I'll be unsatisfied. She said masturbation wouldn't help me. I'll look for a victim.

Bailey I never saw this woman in my life. That shit scared the shit outta me. Because remember I caught a glimpse of Him literally turning me over to this monstrous person, and I was in a dark place in my life. I couldn't hear Him, so He sent somebody that I would and could hear. I felt like He was talking to me. Remember I told you it was a spiritual setup that's behind this.

Bailey, I'll continue to ask God to soften your heart, to grant you the knowledge, wisdom and understanding of who he is and to show you your value and worth in him. I pray that he begins to saturate you with his love, to bless you and show you favor with those whom you come in contact with. Remember I'm here for you!

Alec Johnson

KNUCKLE BUSTER

Bailey

What's up my friend? Things here have been truly hectic! But guess what? I'm okay!! I am good, my friend. I got my job back, and I'm active again. My knees may protest but the "show must go on."

I was thinking about childhood stories that I could share with you that wouldn't be depressing or negative. I will tell you about the summers I lived with my great grandmother. I was almost 8 years old. She lived right next to the "Sportsman" club where there was drinking, drugs and God knows what else that went on all night, every night, but it never spilled over to her house. At least not that I know of.

My "granny" was not mobile at all. She went from the bed to the couch and, at least once a day, to the bathroom. Each morning, I would wake up and make breakfast, which was biscuits that I made from scratch, bacon, syrup again made from scratch, and grits. I did this every morning, and I would prepare dinner also, but at least once each week I could be counted on to burn the beans! Pinto beans took sooo long to cook that I would inevitably forget about them! And the thing is that once I became an adult I forgot how to cook! Even to this day, I fantasize about cooking more easily than I could grab a pan and actually cook something more complicated than eggs or some type of pasta or rice.

But those days are still vivid in my mind. Each Wednesday morning at about 7am I would have to wake up, take all sheets off the beds, and throw them and all clothes worn that week into the bathtub and wash them! Using a scrub board no less! Have you ever seen a scrub board, Bailey? I heard it called a knuckle buster and have never heard a more appropriate name for it. All whites were washed separately, and into the rinse *water I had to add something called "bluing," which is a blue liquid added to the rinse water before the clothes are put in. I have not heard of bluing in many, many years and can't find too many people who've heard of it let alone used it. But it was a part of my growing up and a memory I have to this day.*

> *Your friend,*
> *Floyd*

DEAR MOTHER

Fast moving streams flow like broken dreams
Remember the days all I wanted to be was a cup?
Next I wanted to be mommy's marine?
What a sweet dream

You know as a child I dreamt cute

Then I was demanding, disappointing, and mean
Let me ask you
Did you dream you would adopt and raise a kid this
  disillusioned and broken
Now as a man I know what flows quicker than a
  mothers dreams.
Your tears flow more openly and freely
Than the fastest moving stream

Which was worse, my dreams or Dr. Kings?

Rest his soul. If his dream was broken, what would
  that mean?
It means no pain, no anger, no resentment, no emotion
His soul is at ease
I'm alive. I see the streams of my disappointment,
  failure, and anger.
What can I do to ease the pain?
I don't have many options and, in prison, minimal
  means
Mother, what happened to my dreams?

I'm not a child
My eyes no longer create a stream
I'm a mind detached from my soul
I'm not a child
Angry at life

Desperate to dream
I'm a man

And my heart screams.

By Damien Lanson

FOR STARTERS, LOVE

Bailey,

How've you been since we last wrote one another? I think that's very admirable of you to take him into your home. What happened? How old is he, and what is his name?

I'm curious. Are you really married, or was that a defense mechanism? Once again, I'm only curious because I find you to be remote and kinda standoffish. And it's nothing wrong with that because you have a heart, and you have feelings. More times than not they've both been taken for granted.

Are you truly happy Bailey?

Well, like I told you in my last letter, my aim with you is to open your closed book. It's like you have twenty chains wrapped around your pretty little self, and every time I unlock two, four more start to take form.

So what's life been like since I've heard from you? Your little brother came to stay, and you've been homeschooling him. How's it going?

Yes I have some crazy stories, and I have some painful ones as well. Did I tell you that my father raped my mom, and that's how I was conceived? I find that to be one of those fucked up experiences in my life that moves me to be great for my future existence.

I have a little brother also, and as with you, I pretty much raised mine. His father got murdered in 2000 or 2002. I always got them mixed up. Well, he was the only father I knew, and from the age of 6-9 he abused me physically, emotionally, and mentally because I wasn't his biological son. Crazy right? My mom couldn't really help me cause she was strung out on crack cocaine. I don't really know how, but he had connections in the "CPS." But he took sole custody of me. I remember I used to beg for my mom to come and save me, but she never did. Well not until he got murdered, and that's when she told me he wasn't my father and who really was.

That's when I started going through the psychological problems.

Bailey I didn't really have a good time as a kid and that shit pushes me today so when I do have kids and/or find a woman with kids I know how much love to give them and that's unconditional . . . There should never be a limit to the affection you show a child and woman.

Before I go any further I'm grateful that you write me and TBH I smiled when I got your letter it made me feel good that you care enough to write me. It made my day Bailey.

You asked me what could've been something I think that would've helped me. Well for starters love . . . I never really felt loved as a young child and that was something that made it hard for me to deal with things like school, friends, girlfriends etc . . . I was just a very angry and lonely child.

I hope that you can truly understand my feelings.

Abraham Johnson

FACTS ABOUT TRAUMA

There is no question that repeated traumatic experiences over time impact our ability to function in the world. Research shows having four or more ACES means you are:

- ❖ 2.5 times more likely to be diagnosed with cancer or lung cancer
- ❖ 3.7 times more likely to have anxiety
- ❖ 4.4 times more likely to have chronic depression
- ❖ 4.5 times more likely to develop Alzheimers
- ❖ 5.6 times more likely to engage in illicit drug use
- ❖ 5.8 times more likely to have problematic alcohol use
- ❖ 7.5 times more likely to experience violence victimization in adulthood
- ❖ 15 times more likely to attempt suicide
- ❖ 1,350% more likely to face opiate abuse
- ❖ 7 times more likely to go to prison

While we only find people experiencing this level of trauma in 15.8% of the general population in the United States, 78.1% of the prison population has four or more ACES.[5]

JUVENESCENCE

My correspondence with people who are incarcerated was initially sparked by a desire to figure out what can be done to help struggling teenagers. In order to hear from recent high school graduates, I mainly wrote people between the ages of 18 and 23. Hearing the experiences of these young men helped me understand what it's like to commit crime during this phase of life.

It is widely accepted that teenagers are having a different experience from the rest of us. Ask most parents, and they will tell you their teenager seems to be living in a different reality. Rapidly changing bodies and brains surging with hormones affect their reward and emotional stimuli processing and their ability to reason.[1] Hormones cause the behavior we so strongly associate with being a teenager including aggression, risk-taking, sensation seeking, and a sensitivity to reward. High testosterone and low cortisol levels can also cause delinquent behavior.[2] Teenagers are not able to make rational decisions as well as adults (and even adults struggle with this). The way hormone levels affect teenagers has been studied extensively but not implemented in how we actually treat them in our society. Though we know much about this subject, teenagers are not given the support or forgiveness they need to thrive in our world. This is especially hard for teenagers who were not adequately supported as children, which makes up most of the prison population.[3]

We sometimes refer to a person's experience of fitting in as peer pressure. Looking back at my own life, I see how my desire to fit in and be liked drove me to do things I would never have done on my own. There was so much I did that I didn't enjoy but used as a way to fit in. Still, being a "bad" teenager became a part of my identity then. That overwhelming teenage desire to fit in takes up a lot of space in a person. Based on my experience getting to know people in prison, I believe this longing to be accepted serves as an explanation for an enormous amount of time spent behind bars.

I could have easily ended up in prison during my teenage years. I spent my high school years trying to gain freedom from my parents and validation from everyone else. I see now that my brain was not developed. I was truly unable to reason, and I struggled to cope with the personal challenges I faced. I broke the law as a teenager. Many times. Though I knew it was a possibility then, I now recognize the reality that I could have been incarcerated and could still be in jail today. I did not deserve years of prison time. What I needed was a little redirection and time to grow up. To get away from the circumstances I was raised in. To heal.

My experience as a teenager taught me to have compassion for people who have struggled and made mistakes. During those years, I was homeless, an alcoholic, a drug user, and I did a lot of awful and illegal things. Those experiences gave me the ability to see past a person's actions and inquire about what happened to them. In a way, it made all the struggle worth it, though I would never choose to go through those experiences again.

I see this same kind of forgiving attitude in the people I write. They give me so much grace. When I share awful things I have done, they ask meaningful questions like, "What were you going through during that time that pushed you to make that decision? Do you feel you've healed from this experience?" I don't meet many people in their early twenties who ask such kind and insightful questions. But my pen pals do. My correspondence with many of my pen pals makes me wonder why they are still in prison. I do not mean what they are incarcerated for. I mean why they are still locked up when they have the ability and such a strong desire to make better choices.

Sending people to prison as teenagers is baffling. We should expect for them to go through a hard time, not always understanding the consequences of their actions. We should *prepare* for this behavior in teenagers. We should have a system that addresses what's actually happening inside of them instead of locking them away hoping they will figure it out and not become part of the huge number of people who continue committing crimes, spending most of their lives locked behind bars. Because a huge portion of crime is committed by people who have an undeveloped brain. Outside of gambling, most crimes are committed by people under the age of 25.[4]

I am here to bear witness to the fact that there is a place for everyone in society. We do belong here. I have gotten to know these men and seen the truth of who they are. They are people with the same needs, wants, and desires that all of us have. If we slow down long enough to listen to their stories, solutions may begin to surface.

I DON'T ALWAYS MAKE THE RIGHT CHOICE

Dear Bailey,

First I would like to say, wow! I highly applaud you for taking responsibility of three kids lives plus one of your own. Being 23 that's a lot to take on. Like you, I wish people would take care of their children. But instead they want to abuse them, starve them, and abandon them. I'm 22 with no kids, but I almost had one. The woman who was pregnant had a miscarriage. I would have dropped everything to make sure my child wanted for nothing. Kids are not disposable play toys that once you get tired of them you throw them to the curb. That is why there are so many young people locked up right now. Like me. My mom gave me 1 rule: don't bring trouble to the house. That's not a way to raise a kid. Still, I love my mother because without her I would not be here.

My plans after high school? Hm . . . I'm going to be honest with you. I am surprised I made it so far. My neighborhood was so bad that I fell victim to the gang life, selling drugs and other things. So even though I was in sports, I honestly was not thinking that far ahead. My little brother was killed in a gang-related shooting. My mom was strung out, so I was getting food any way I could. I did not know my life expectancy, but I can tell you about now. I want to open a tattoo shop and start a record label. I have a business mind.

What do I wish I learned? I wish I learned problem solving in real life situations. I mean I don't have a problem, but when I get mad, I dont always make the right choice. (I don't know if that counts.) What were the effects of not knowing? Well, for one I ended up locked up because of not thinking things through when I was mad. I wish I could go back and redo my whole high school experience. I would take everything more serious and really try my hardest to graduate and go on to college under a football scholarship.

Logan Brooks

THE STRUGGLE IS REAL

Dear Bailey,

I'm very glad to know I could convey my past experiences in a way that can touch your heart. I have to say when I hear of someone being a foster parent I have a new level of respect for them. I know as a mother of foster children you have done your research on what to expect . . . My story is like maybe some of your adopted kids? I lost my parents because they were living too fast of a life—drugs, gangs, and other habits that you shouldn't have as a parent. The state ended up taking me away. My full-blood brother and I both got taken away by the state. The state split us up and put us both into different foster homes. He was all I had. And I was all he had. The struggle is real I'm telling you. At the end of the day, sometimes we are born into demise and sometimes we create our own.

I remember I was in kindergarten, and the school I went to had more white kids then African Americans. I used to go through hell everyday. It sounds like a movie, but I have no need to embellish my story. I used to get spit on. These two twins William and Brockton. I ended up fighting them and hurting one of them, and they brought me to the principal's office. Mr. Melody, he tried to threaten me by calling my foster parents. He wanted to know why I fought them and I wouldn't tell him. Finally, he called my foster dad, and I said what happened. Mr. Melody hung up and tried telling me, "That is no reason to hurt somebody Cornelius." My birth name is Cornelius.

Did you never meet someone who you can't be open with because either they will judge you or be of no help or have too many problems of their own to try to understand yours? There is too much hurt in this world.

If you haven't heard the song "Where is the love" by the Black Eyed Peas listen to it. It is the truth.

I have lived in a lot of places with a lot of different people. I've been incarcerated since I was 20, but I've lived all over the place. Almost all those places were predominantly white. Living and going to school in those places was hard. One place I lived, I went to sign up for sports. The athletic board wouldn't let me play. In Washington, 4A is the biggest. They have 2000+ kids, and the school I transferred to had 500+. They made me have a big hearing three times to determine if I was eligible. They thought the school that I was going to recruited me for athletic purposes. They didn't. All the people at my hearing were old white farmers who were the coaches of my competing teams. They denied me. Prior to that I played football at a big school. I had started on varsity ever since my sophomore year. I got letters from a few small D2 colleges for football and track. The board interviewing me knew it, so they denied me twice. The 3rd time we appealed, we had to call the "WIAA." They approved me because I told them about my living situation.

Prior to moving there I went on a spree and shot at people, and somebody I ended up getting. A week and a half later, I went to a party. I'm linked up with my bro in Idaho, and I'm running this broad not knowing I been set up by my best friend. I walk out the back door I see my homies whip in the cup so I take literally one step off the porch, get cracked by a baseball bat and get stomped out. I couldn't fight back cause it happened WAY too fast, long story short I didn't have my pistol. I got my eyebrow split open. My jaw was split on three sides. It was literally hanging so broke I couldn't close it. Instead of killing those dudes I chalked it up to the game. That was my karma for what happened last week. Being betrayed by my brother/best friend I said fuck it once I got my jaw wired shut I dipped outta town that's how I ended up moving. Anyway, they made it a point to cast me out. When I had my hearing in front of the board this teacher named Todette was supposed to help me, so I told her my life story. Obviously I left out some stuff that was not needed to be known. But this broad is supposed to keep it confidential. A week later her son is telling everybody I'm a bad person. I do drugs and deal drugs. I carry a gun and all this stuff. All these kids is squares at my school. It's a farm town. All they have guns for is to hunt. I'm from the city where people hunt people not animals. And if you don't have that tool and you have squeezed on somebody, and they see you, you are history, especially if you don't have a tool. "Only a fool puts in work but doesn't carry his tool."

Bailey, you and I both know the education system lacks diversity. That being said, how can you expect the school system to help kids? It can't. I truly believe the school system needs a way to target kids home life better. School isn't where it starts. My schooling from 3rd to 12th grade no lie was first daycare so momma don't gotta deal with me. Then, it became the kick it spot in middle school. Kick it, smoke weed, n hump on the girls then in highschool it was a place to sell drugs. All business. You hear more gossip in the school than you do the streets. Teachers don't care if a mexican or nigga don't pass or drop out. They expect it. Especially in a big school they don't have enough programs or teachers to individually help students. Don't get me wrong you have some dedicated and devoted teachers, but at the end of the night, if my teacher don't care I don't either.

When I was on the concrete, nothing I learned in high school helped me do road construction or fish. None of that helped me when I was in the Army. The school system teaches not even the basics. Nowadays it's a place where you link up with your homies before school, get high, drink a lil, meet some women, run um during your free period or at lunch, then go to PE, and call it a day. It's a circus. I used to literally hit my teacher's assistant up on Snapchat. She was 25. I'd tell her to slide thru, and we would drink, and then I'd knock it down. Mind you I might have had a unique experience, but I know I'm not the only student who did those things. Look, in my time nobody cared. You wanna kick me out of school? Ok. I can go to alternative school and get my GED in three months. They used to give me all my tests verbally in school because I couldn't read or write. They wondered why I was failing and falling behind. Then my foster mom said give them to him orally, and I aced all of them.

Could you agree children are a product of their environment and education? When I was in elementary the school didn't know how to handle me. I'm having girlfriends, already teaching them things. I'm flooding the urinal and having fun like it's Chuck E Cheese—typical class clown. So the school thought they came up with an ingenious plan. Whenever Cornelius starts acting up, send him to the special ed room, and let him play by himself and think about why he's down there. I'd be down there hours while everybody else is learning how to write cursive and learning how to read. All the time I didn't care. They didn't call my parents cause they was scared they would beat on me. So everyday for 3+ years they would send me home with a smiley face sticker to show I had a good day. At the time it was lovely. Me and my first love, Lacresha, got to be down there all day playing house. She was in the same living situation as me, so whenever I was having a bad day they would pull her out of class, and we would play house and talk. But how beneficial is that in the long run? I'm losing out on my education because you don't have the proper training or knowledge to handle someone like me right?

It's not all their fault. Nobody is perfect. I can't hold resentment to any individuals. When I was in 4th grade I was sitting in mandatory music class. I hated it. Only cool part was all the women in it. So I'm in class poppin it at these girls and my music teacher tried kicking me out. I said "No, I promise I won't talk again." I didn't wanna get kicked outta his class because I knew he would call my dad, and I'd get my ass beat when I got home, so I refused. I was begging him, so this dude teacher picked me up by the throat and threw me out the classroom. The girl I was poppin it at told the principal what happened. I came back the next day with fingernail marks and bruises on my neck. So mind you the girl, Lucy, told the principal he asked to see me. I went in and saw him. I didn't even tell my parents the full story because I knew they would come to school turn't up. So I told the principal exactly what happened then Lucy came in and told the same story. I showed him the marks. He told me, "You're lying. Mr. Rumbolt has been working here for years, and we have never had this issue."

They put me back in his class, and his weird ass failed me. For the longest time they put me in special ed. Not like IEP. They put me in with the mentally handicapped. They tried diagnosing me with aspergers and some other shit. Then, they completely took me out of class and put me in the library. The librarian was in LOVE with me. She got me into books, and I started reading a lot. Then, by 6th grade when I could read I was at a 13th grade reading level. They quickly changed my diagnosis. They had the audacity to tell me I wasn't "as stupid as I made myself seem. I was just oppositional defiant," so then, when I seriously couldn't do something right such as math, I wouldn't even try. They would grill me. Send me to in-school suspension. Make me come in early and stay late after school.

After all that bullshit, the school recommended my foster family take me to health care specialists. It was hell. I literally remember every health care specialist I had. One hood doctor, I got baked by him. He recommended medication that was horrible. Shit had me like a zombie. I wasn't diagnosed with PTSD when I was younger but that's what they thought I had because I was in a lot of different homes and seen and been through a lot of abuse. My brother got his leg broken by my "parents" when we was babies. We were starved, neglected, and abused. We weren't nothing to nobody but a nuisance. But seriously, don't take pity for that is almost every kid born in the hood. Schools are quick to have a parent have their child checked out. Too many people set their expectations to an unreachable standard. Nobody is like you. Nobody is like me. Yes, some people may look as attractive as us, but nobody's mind and heart is the same complexity as ours. How can you judge someone's aptitude based on the dry material you mandate them to read? That creates lethargic, unmotivated students. At this point I've gotten way off topic. I'm going to end this letter. May Allah bless you.

Damien Lanson

KID AT HEART

Bailey,

I got your letter. I would like to say thank you. I really appreciate you writing me. It's good to know that there are still kind people in the world trying to make a difference in the lives of others.

And here is something for you. When I was 5 or 6, I was having behavioral problems. My grandmother took me to a psychiatrist, and long story short, I was diagnosed with ADHD and prescribed adderall. At 5 years old! From that point on, I was always seeing the "doctors," and they always tinkered with my medication. I look back now, and I think all I needed was somebody to talk to about why I felt the way I felt and why I behaved the way I did. My grandparents tried to talk to me, but I couldn't trust them. The psychs tried to pry into my mind, but I was especially closed and guarded against them. I didn't trust them ever. What I needed was someone I considered an equal, a peer, that also did the same as me, that I wouldn't fear reprisal from.

If I would have had a parent or grandparent where my trust was not broken, a person that I could just say how I felt without fear of what they'll do to punish me, I would have a completely different psychological makeup.

Children, I think, should be able to trust their parents! They should have no fear to be able to confide honestly with their family. Unbreakable understanding, the bond between child and parent should be strong enough that the child can honestly discuss openly without judgment or fear of reprisal. Perhaps only then can all the bullshit be set aside, and true progress can be made.

I know if I could have told my folks anything when I was a kid with that certainty maybe I would have been able to deal with my feeling of being disconnected.

What good is a family that cannot even properly communicate with each other? No good at all. I would guess it would take self control on behalf of the parent as well as maturity in the child to recognize such a bond. Because when something can be discussed without fear and with open mindedness, the child might be able to help the parent understand better exactly what can be done to stop. Fear caused me to hold back. A family that cannot establish that bond in my opinion is unhealthy. Dysfunctional. A joke. I know because that's what I lived in, and you too Bailey. You know. You've been there. It's good to know that I'm not alone in that. I feel like I can keep it real with you. I feel so much better when I write to you. You know how it feels. To an extent, you are one who could possibly relate.

Do you know how hard it is for me to write my family a letter as RAW and sincere as this? It feels like a necessary evil when I write them. I could never tell them the shit I tell you. I'd have them believe they gave me the best damn childhood a kid could have, let them take it to their grave. It would break my grandparents hearts if I told them otherwise. Honestly, they did the best they could given the circumstances. But you know how it is, I still love them. I think the fact that I still praise their "unconditional" love, and I don't convey resentment to them, I think that makes it harder on them. I just want them to go peacefully. I know, me incarcerated and the events that led up to me being jailed is all me, my fault, but they know that they did play a part in the sentence I got. My pap will never forgive himself, Bailey. It eats away at his heart, that he, in fact, allowed an illegal search and seizure without a warrant, and he'll never forgive himself for signing that paper. That I could have beat my case. He didn't know at the time though. They tricked him. I love my grandfather Bailey. He was the closest thing to an actual father I ever had. Him and I are both silently hoping I get paroled before he dies. I wouldn't be able to forgive myself if I couldn't make it home to him in time.

Why am I incarcerated? Because I am a fool and almost took a man's life in a drug deal gone wrong. Desperation and addiction are two words for it. There is so much Bailey. Just know that it helps me to write you. And I'm still a kid at heart. So at least you can safely say you helped me. So thanks once again. Keep your head up, player! Haha.

Izaak Shunk

DESTINED

Okay, Bailey. Here you go.

High school. It's a blur. No good memories. At this point I'm so past high school it's ridiculous. I'm only 4 years removed from graduating and I feel like it's been decades. History, Math, English . . . All that stuff means nothing to me today. What I wish they would have taught me was what was going on in my head and why couldn't I stop it. I was crippled with social anxiety and depression in my teenage years. I was alone in a world where everyone was connecting around me. I'm surprised at how rarely I contemplated suicide during these times. I was lost. And no math or no physics could help me find my way.

Now? 4 years later? I never think about high school. Jail and prison are my high school. In the 6 years I got left, I intend to learn as much as I can from my surroundings. Why? Because I'm destined to. I wouldn't be here if I wasn't.

I don't want to hurt anybody. I've never even been in a fist fight. I'm an artist. A poet. A visionary. Stuck in the land where there is no vision. Only reality. And that only makes my vision stronger. I want my perspective to bring joy to everybody. Not today, but one day it will. It's my mission.

Francisco Gutierrez

YOU JUST ADAPT

Hi Bailey,

I am 22 years old, and I am a father of one. I dropped out at the age of 15. I am incarcerated for murder. After high school, I was really planning on working hard to make my own carpentry company. That's what I enjoy doing. I have a passion for it.

I really wish I had learned how to value life! How special our freedom is. If I would have learned that, I wouldn't be in this lonely, cold cell right now. Now I'm here in the penitentiary wasting 17 years of my life. Trying to change, but it's hard cause of the environment we're in. I'm trying not to get institutionalized, but you know, sooner or later, you just adapt to your surroundings. You know I'm gang affiliated. It's just a prison gang. It's hard down here in prison; this is not a fun place to be in.

I really hope all those kids out there fulfill their dreams and reach their goals in life. Life can be really, really tough, but we just need to be strong and pursue our purpose. I hope to hear back from you.

Much respect,
Donavon Mendez

THE REASON I DID THIS

Hi Bailey,

I'm 22 years old. I grew up with no dad. Only my mom, and I guess it's true it ain't easy for a woman to raise a man. I can't really tell you about high school other than I got out of juvenile after doing 2 years. My dad came back, and he had AIDS, so I just beat him up. I stole cars at a young age, thirteen. The reason I did this was to help my family. I would leave for 2-3 months so I could make some money. I'd make $1500 to $3000 a day, but I had my own little habits. I've been doing heroin since I was eleven. I did $300 of heroin a day, and after a while I got into bars. It's crazy. I learned how to drive from stealing cars. I got put into a stolen car by my OG. He said just drive the speed and just keep our eyes out for the cops. Don't worry the car ain't going to hit the stolen list till 24 hours. If you get locked up, don't say shit, just chill, and they let you go in 3-4 months on probation. I just ran in my hood with my gang laying down anyone. By laying down I mean rob them, beat them up, putting in work, put people down in the gang, take niggas out the gang. I got so involved, I forgot why I got into this life—to help my family. Now I'm just another gang member. Crazy. I'll keep writing as long as you want me to.

Best wishes and regards,
Carlos Miranda

LEARN TO LAUGH

Bailey,

I just received the book that you sent me the other day and I wanted to thank you deeply for thinking of me and sending it. It's one of the nicest things anyone's done for me in a long time so I just really wanted you to know that I appreciate it. Not only that but I've been reading it. I'm only on chapter four because I've been taking the time to take notes and really try to put into practice what the book is trying to teach. Honestly it's already having small impacts on me everyday. Just in the ways I think and approach certain aspects of my day. It got me to stop putting off this project I've been meaning to get started on for the longest time, so really Bailey, thank you.

Well, growing up was rough. My parents divorced when I was young and used to put my four siblings and I in the middle of everything. I lost a lot of respect for both of them during their custody battle because I felt like they were being selfish. So after their divorce, I never really listened to much they had to tell me. Everything I learned after that was really by trial and error. A lot of errors. My community was and to this day is filled with gang activity and violence. Seeing people hurt, jumped on, or even shot became habitual. I was numb to it. The guys on the corner slowly became the people I looked up to. They had everything I wanted. Money, girls, respect, and they acted as if they were family. But my parents wouldn't let me chill with them. They'd barely even let me leave the front yard.

At this time, I was splitting the week in half living with my dad at his mother's house and my mom at her mother's. Both were apartments within a couple blocks of each other, both government financed buildings, and both in the middle of the ghetto. Now, my parents *wouldn't let me hang out with the guys from my area, but my father would chill with them all the time. Would make sure to shake up with them when we were passing by. Would even make sure they knew who his children were so they'd never mess with us. Later on I'd learn that my father used to be one of those guys hanging out on the corner and still had a level of respect from both the older and younger generation of neighborhood thugs.*

By the age of twelve, my father was incarcerated. My two older brothers had moved out by now and lived on their own. Essentially, I was the man of the house, so while my mom was working full-time and my grandmother was watching the little ones, I would take advantage and hang out in the streets all day. The same guys my father stopped me from being around were the exact ones I chilled with everyday now. The ones I looked up to. Who I thought had all the answers to my problems. They were the ones who taught me how to take from others, how to get fast money, fast girls, and how to get respect and love in my neighborhood. They put the first blunt I ever smoked to my lips and the first gun I ever held in my hands. That's the influence my community had on me. It made me value the people I had to prove myself to instead of the ones who loved me unconditionally. It conditioned me to be quick to violence, because the more violent you are, the more respect you have.

It taught me how to hurt others in order to stop my own pain. I've been through my fair share. Poverty, from sleeping on floors to sleeping in cars. Show up to school in the same clothes as yesterday and fight anyone who had something to say about it. I've been jumped on, have knife wounds, and have dodged bullets. I've even fallen in love and had my heart broken believe it or not. That's another story though. But you learn to laugh at the pain.

Through it all, I've realized what love really is and who's really by my side. How to stay out of trouble and think for myself. How to carry myself as a man. What and who is important in my life. Probably the most important thing that I've learned is that it's never too late to change, to grow, or to learn. How have I grown? I look at life through a different lens than I used to. Every day is a chance to learn. To work on myself. Mind, body, and spirit. I value love, happiness, trust, honesty, and loyalty instead of money and sex. My mind has gotten sharper and my heart softer. I've grown to love myself and learned exactly who I want to become, which is a better man tomorrow then I was today. I've repaired bonds with everyone in my family. If you knew the child I used to be and saw today the man I've become, you probably wouldn't believe the difference. Thank you for taking the time to really get to know me Bailey. It means a lot.

Luca Pacheco

SEARCHIN FOR CHANGE

Dear Bailey,

I know this letter will be a surprise for sure. You don't know me and, of course, are wondering how I got your information. Well, Donavon Mendez is a good friend of mine. We were talking one day about books, and your name came up. So I will tell you about myself to give you an idea about me.

I grew up very rough, back and forth from the streets of Northern California to Central Texas. Raised by a mother of five who was always working long hours. I, being the oldest, was left to take care of the kids. Money was always a problem because we barely had enough money to cover the bills, so food became something that always came up short. This would bother me because I hated to see my younger brothers and sister hungry, so just to feed them, I would steal frozen dishes from the store. They were flat, and I could put them in my stomach, part tucked in my pants, and feed everyone. I would also go fishing to try and catch fish, but that wouldn't always work. I was eleven years old at this time.

I started to become a kid the gang members liked because growing up poor, I always had to fight in school because my shoes were cheap and worn out. They embraced me with ease. They gave me drugs, and I would sell to support myself and help my mom out. At sixteen, I moved out on my own and was well-connected from Austin, Texas to Dallas where I was getting my drugs from. School was always a priority for me. It was something I enjoyed but did not know my full potential. I quit my sophomore year and got my GED, so I wouldn't have to attend school anymore.

As my reputation was building in the streets, I was arrested and sent to prison at 18. During that time in prison, I met more people and became part of what is now the most dangerous prison gang in Texas. I was going to give you the name, but it could stop this letter from reaching you. So now with power, I was released in 2012 after serving four years. The next day after I was released, I called people all over Texas and started to get myself back established. Six months later in September 2012, I was raided and sent back to prison. This is when I started to learn about myself and my full potential. Two years ago, I got out of the gang life and took the worst beating of my life, but it was well worth it. Since then, I've studied different religions, and I found peace in Islam, so I'm a muslim today. For me, it's a sense of peace that I've needed for a long time. Although I no longer have the things I used to, I'm at peace with myself through the grace of God.

Now that you have learned about me somewhat, I hope that you feel more comfortable reading further. Where I believe society goes wrong: mainly in the minority part for one. Also, that school is based on academics. What about life skills for those who don't have the correct guidance at home? We need more people out there telling their stories in schools in the roughest parts of the country. Society makes it to where if you know what is good for you, cool. If not, well we will make money off you by the justice system, and it's a never-ending cycle. Even prison is meant for you to fail. I had to learn through books I stumbled across after people threw them out of their cell, maybe because they're just ignorant towards changing their life around. Prison is the best school for learning how to come back. That's the truth, and there's no other way to put it.

In my spare time, I write business plans. I try to write as much of my thoughts on paper as I can because I read that when you do this, you're most likely to accomplish what you desire to do. Also so I can have them to take home with me as a blueprint for what is to come after years of planning. The next step is freedom in order to capitalize on what I'm dedicated to do.

Everyone in life can become whatever they want; they just have to have the guidance. When you leave a child to make his own decisions without someone to tell them the outcome, they are left to fail. I seen it in myself growing up because I've compared my decision making today and where I was before. There were no plans after high school. I was just living for the moment. That's why I say we need more guidance and tools to help us who are less fortunate. Who don't have parents to provide us with time of their own. I wish I had learned more about myself from someone who could tell me more than what I was good at. In order to achieve it, you're going to have to polish your skills and set yourself up to become successful. I also wish I knew about things after high school such as military, police academy, working for the state, life insurance, retirement, IRA, etc. The list is long. The effects that come from not knowings leads to the things you do know, which are gangs and easy money such as robbery, selling drugs, extortion, and basic street life.

If public school was in my hands, I would teach a class on statistics—on everything from the graduation rate to the incarceration rate according to city and state. I would also raise awareness through motivational speakers from all over the world who could show students they can achieve whatever they choose to in life. No one should ever have to worry about paying for school or anything like that, but it's reality. We should teach people about other opportunities. Upon my release, I want to give people a fighting chance. The chance I didn't have. I really want to tell my story to the world. Maybe we can help each other. I'll leave you with a poem I wrote when I was 16 in a 3-month juvenile boot camp.

I was raised in these streets with nothing but pain
Asking God can he help me because I'm searchin for change.
Just wanting to make a profit and make it legit
Because everyday in the ghetto there's a life that's spent.
So let me tell you the truth I've been concealing from God
Caught up in situations try'n to get on my job
And yes, it's a shame how I'm motivated by the struggle and pain
But that's the way that I was raised, and had to be raised
the game.

One more thing that I don't understand is why people trip on religion
Cause we all serve on God in this life that we're given.

This is the mind of a 16 year old who wants a real life but doesn't know it exists. May you be blessed in all you do in life.

Salizar Webb

THE CONTROLLED VARIABLE

Dear Bailey,

I am 23 years old as of April 22nd. I am currently incarcerated for a rape charge and sex-abuse charge it sounds worse than it is. Its stigma is negative. Upon graduating high school I still maintained a relationship with a girl who was 14 while I was 18. I ended up getting her pregnant, and the parents pressed charges. The parents tried dropping the charges, and I went to trial, but the state of Oregon took the case and baked it, like double baked. Hopefully, I can still be of use despite my charges.

I used to enjoy late nights with my friends, my cat, being outdoors, driving, and working out. Those are the main things I enjoyed. Freedom, Bailey. Where did I struggle, wow!! That's a pretty broad question. To be exact I struggled from birth, from the womb, straight into foster care. My life struggle has been with my race and also with my lack of guidance. Like science, the controlled variable was myself, and the manipulated variable was parents, family, towns, and friends. I have never been stable for over 1 ½ years. I connected with very few teachers. People were quick to judge my lifestyle. Some of the places I lived I was automatically looked down on. One, I'm a mixed African American. Two, I'm a troubled child with no structure. Teachers were quick to send me to the principal or quick to fail me and sometimes openly show their contempt. Most of my conflicts, Bailey, were racially motivated because of where I was living. As you know, nothing separates a teacher's mentality from a student's. Only difference is credentials and age. Believe me, teachers and educators are sometimes just as ignorant as students. In all truth, I graduated because they didn't want to take me. My senior year I literally had all free periods. I took weightlifting, English, and government. They passed me in all other classes.

The problem with the system, I believe, is it lacks individuality. There were people like me who never learned how to write or read even when that's all you do in school. And no teacher took the time out to individually help me. I never got taught algebra in school. They passed me on all the tests, so my limit is long division (lol).

My plans after high school were to move like anybody who doesn't have solidarity or guidance. I got a travel case from my high school office clerk, packed it, and went to alaska. College was not an option. I have no clue how to enroll or get money for loans. So I just stacked money and wanted to travel the world. After Alaska I enlisted in the Army. I wish I had learned real skills in school that could help me in the real world. The school system proctors best to people who have enough stability to go to college. I knew I was gonna come to prison, not for this charge. I was thinking attempted murder and murder. I wish they could have told me what life would be like for someone who didn't go to college. I'm not the only kid that grew up with no dad or mom in the city with violence, drugs, gangs and low hope. So what I really wish I learned was how to conduct myself as a man. The effects of me not knowing are simply a lack of motivation. Teachers would tell me, Damien you're gonna end up in prison or my favorite, Damien, you need to go to college. If you don't, you won't be able to earn a living. Lack of proper motivation is the effect.

Damien Lanson

P.S. It took me going to prison to get to college. Currently I attend college at Adams State University. Its mail based correspondence. I just got done with sociology. I have been in the hole for 100+ days. I get out in 17. May this letter reach you in good health, Bailey.

I WOULDN'T BE IN PRISON

Hey Bailey,

My name is Tyrone. I'm 23 years of age. I'm locked up for armed robbery and aggravated vehicular hijacking. I would blame my environment to play a part of that more than my high school. The only thing is the school was so big that I didn't feel in place. There was no connections between the teachers and me. In fact, I found myself in arguments with a lot of them like my geometry teacher, for instance. She wanted to pick an argument with me everyday no matter what I did. So by me feeling a certain type of way, a sense of not belonging, I would leave school early, go back to the old neighborhood, and play the streets. I got arrested when I was 16 years old, so right before I finished my sophomore year. Plus in that school I don't remember having any black teachers. I did have one teacher who was concerned about where I was heading. She was genuine and naturally a good person. Everything I've learned has been in prison. Maybe certain things I didn't learn in school was because of me being disengaged due to personal reasons, but the school didn't have no one that made me feel comfortable. I would go to the guidance office and talk to the counselor but would feel him judging me. I just didn't feel welcomed in school. I wish I did because I strongly feel like if I was, I wouldn't be in prison. I would probably be playing basketball at one of these colleges somewhere.

I do understand that I missed out on a lot of opportunities, but everything happens for a reason. Like me meeting you. I hope to hear from you soon.

Sincerely,
Tyrone Sampson

DEAD IN A CASKET OR LOCKED IN A CELL

Hi Bailey,

My first and last high school that I attended, I was only there for nearly a month. At that time, I had gotten arrested and put in Juvenile for a felony charge.

During my incarceration in the juvenile system, I kept on going to school until the end of my sentence and made it all the way to the 11th grade. When I received parole, I had a lot of responsibilities and couldn't go back to school because of my criminal history. Today, I'm incarcerated for 1st degree felony murder charge. Went to trial on self-defense and the judge sentenced me to 45 years concurrent with my juvenile time as well with an appeal to this sentence.

When I was younger I enjoyed going out a lot with friends, reading urban novels, and listening to music. Growing up, I struggled a lot from gang-activity, racial fights, police, drugs and "communication." My teachers always were a problem to me, mainly for that they would always sit there in front of the class and tell me, "You're gonna end up dead in a casket or locked up in a cell." Sure enough they were right.

My plan after high school was I wanted to serve for the U.S. Marines, discharge my little 5 years, work my way into the medical field. I wish I would have learned the knowledge and wisdom that I know now because growing up, I never had guidance and advice and always learned the hard way. I wish the best blessings and high spirits. Till pen and paper meet again.

Your realest friend.
Sincerely,
Antonio Alvarez

TURNING POINT

Bailey,

I am very happy to hear from you. I was so excited to see your name on the envelope. I was smiling very very hard. It's rare that men like me in my current situation meet people like you who care and want to get to know our story, our lives, and our upbringing, so to have met you is truly a blessing, and I'll cherish it.

I grew up on the east side of Chicago, Illinois. I started out as a class A student in Elementary school and I believe the turning point in my life came when I lost my older brother to "gun violence" when I was 11 years old. I began staying out late and missing school. I ended up catching my very first criminal case at 13 years old in which I spent 11 months in a juvenile detention center and that's where I finished elementary school and graduated to high school. High school was very different for me because I didn't come straight from a public school in Chicago. I came from jail and everyone knew that. They knew that I was there for a violent crime, so my name was always in someone else's conversation. I was considered a well-known person. I was very popular. I did attend all my scheduled classes. I considered myself very respectful to my peers and teachers. I would say all of my troubles and problems were on the outside of school being that I was a part of a gang living in a very violent neighborhood.

I've been incarcerated since I was 16, so if I was given a self-help book at 16, I would've read it because there was so much negativity going on in my life with violence that I wouldn't have thought twice about reading. It was about living or dying and I had to do what I had to do at 16 to make it, and if you ask me if I regret any of it, I'll tell you no because that made me who I am today, and I am a man who has grown a lot over these 12 years.

I am ready to live out in that real world next year. I come home next year, so I am looking forward to applying to a community college. I have been successfully going to school here, but I also want to continue when I do go home.

Thanks again for your words and not forgetting about me. I appreciate you Bailey, and I can't wait to hear from you. Write soon, okay . . .

Write me soon, stay safe.
Sincerely,
Mark Young

I'M ACTUALLY A GOOD PERSON

Hey Bailey,

Glad to hear from you. May I find you at peace and healthy both mentally and physically.

I was in an alternative school before I entered high school due to behavior issues. I went to three high schools. At one there were fights and shootings on school property, so it was pretty easy for someone to get distracted. I got along with my teachers, but I was a bit of a class clown so I didn't connect much with them.

This disinterest started when I started getting involved more with the streets and kept having to change schools because of the foster homes I was in. I was in foster homes from 14 to 16. I've been to 4 different foster homes and every one I had to change schools and make new friends, so it kind of was me giving up adjusting. I was smart so it was more of not wanting to be there.

I was always the type to get good grades, always have. I'd eventually get my grades up bc of football. I was madly in love with the sport! It was a way I thought I could get into college because I was not financially right nor my family. So it was like the only way I thought at the time to get a scholarship.

To be honest, Bailey, sometimes I believe students in high school start to lose interest, especially those in bad neighborhoods when they realize college is the next step and to get into college is a lot of money. I don't know why America charges Americans thousands of dollars to be successful. Once it starts to get closer to college it's like, "Okay, I'm not going to be able to get in, so what's the point?"

I am doing time now for aggravated assault. Being around the wrong people and in a bad environment, but I'm actually a good person with goals and a lot of my goals have to do with helping people and contributing to the helpless and needy. I'm very big on kids and doing whatever it takes to help them go on the right path because I was that kid once.

Have a nice day with your head towards the stars!

Tim Garza

FOOTBALL WAS MY LIFE

Hey Bailey,

I am 23 years old right now. I have been locked up since I was 19 and I get out next year. Me and my mom moved into a 2-bedroom apartment and left my brothers and stepdad at the house just so I could attend this school for their football program. Football was always my life and I am the only person in Arizona football to play freshman JV and varsity in the same year. My mom worked a lot so I kind of had free reign to do whatever I wanted, but I was thriving in athletics and academics so my parents felt like I had earned the right to go out and have fun, I guess.

Throughout high-school me and my friends would shoplift from the mall. It slowly escalated to stealing iphones, ipods, cameras, or cash from backpacks left in the locker rooms, or purses that were unattended at parties. Playing football was a year-round commitment, so none of us had time to get a part-time job, and it was just how we got cash for beer, clothes, and girls. My junior year a friend of mine broke into a house. I was the driver, and we both got charged with burglaries. It feels like that's where my life as I know it "ended."

I was suspended for the year from football so me and my mom moved back with my step dad and brothers. I did my senior year at a small high school there. I was on probation, and I kept smoking weed and failing UAs, so I would regularly have to spend a week or month in juvy. I dropped out of high school after my senior year football season and got my GED in juvy before my 18th birthday.

When I turned 18, I worked construction for a few months (I had a serious girlfriend at the time). Four months or so later I called my old coach and long-story short ended up going to New Mexico to play college ball.

I quit after a few months to come back to my girlfriend in Arizona who broke up with me weeks after I came back. And I kind of went off the deep end, robbed a drug dealer who sold weed, and he called the cops. I was given 5 ½ years for armed robbery. One thing that was cool about the school I played football at was the amount of school spirit and pride everyone had. Our whole school was like a team and pep rallies and all that were really fun. Anyway, I hope to hear from you soon. I wish you the best, be safe, keep your head up, and can't wait to hear back.

Sincerely,
Marcus Joel Davis

DON'T BE IN A RUSH FOR NOTHING

Hey Bailey,

Congratulations on getting married. Four kids? Wow, how do you like being a mother and a wife? I'm 22 and incarcerated for home invasion, trying to rob a guy that had $20,000 of drug money in his house. I wish I learned money 101 skills rather than doing wrong things to get fast money. The main thing I think young people need to know is don't be in a rush for nothing. Take your time growing up. Fast money isn't the right way to go. It leads to prison or death. I have so many childhood friends who are dead before they turn 18 and ever had a chance to experience parenthood or are in prison all for fast money when there's plenty of legal ways to get money.

Until next time.
Jonah Watkins

FACTS ABOUT JUVENESCENCE

Outside of gambling, most crimes are committed by people under the age of 25.[5]

The hormones we experience during puberty are known to cause delinquent behavior.[6]

Gang members are typically between the ages of 12 and 24. The average age for a gang member is 17 to 18 years old.[7]

"The growing consensus among experts was perhaps best reflected by the National Advisory Commission on Criminal Justice Standards and Goals, which issued a recommendation in 1973 that 'no new institutions for adults should be built and existing institutions for juveniles should be closed.' This recommendation was based on their finding that 'the prison, the reformatory and the jail have achieved only a shocking record of failure. There is overwhelming evidence that these institutions create crime rather than prevent it.'"[8] —*The New Jim Crow* by Michelle Alexander

FATHERLESSNESS

Fatherlessness was not a problem I was looking for or expecting, but in our letters, the burden of absent fathers appeared. Desperation welled inside almost every one of my pen pals as they sought a father. Most often, that father was found not in a coach or an uncle but in a gang. I noticed how my pen pals who had a father present in their childhood developed an uncommon resilience and belief in themselves. When I asked my pen pals about these observations, they confirmed my theory. They said most men they meet in prison grew up without a father. They praised their moms, grateful for how hard they worked to put food on the table and step into both roles, but they always shared how their mom could never have filled the role of a father. Not really. And an emptiness formed inside them with a hunger to be filled.

Fatherlessness has been paving the road to crime. Indeed, there is a crisis of fatherless homes in our country. Back in 1999, 72% of the population said that fatherlessness was the most significant family or social problem facing America.[1] The lack of fathers in our country has remained, and the results are shattering people's lives. When we grow up without a parent, there is a deep longing that accumulates in us. A need to be loved, cherished, and guided, to be given a model for how to live.

For a lot of young people who don't have a father, the first person who shows interest in them is really important as that person reveals what they have been looking for: belonging. It is easy to see how young people could end up in gangs when parent and child are divided. A brotherhood of friends who rely on each other is exactly what every teenager wants. Most of us have peer idols we look up to in adolescence. It gives us someone to model ourselves after as we grapple with our identities and serves as a conduit for fitting in with our peers. The problem is that fitting in is the exact opposite of belonging. Brene Brown says that by fitting in, we give up who we really are in order to fit other people's ideas of who we should be. Most teenagers who experience "fitting in" end up feeling more isolated and alone, which is exactly how I felt as a struggling teen surrounded by crime, drugs, and absent parents.

Gang members are typically between the ages of 12 and 24, and the average age for a gang member is 17 to 18 years old.[2] During this time, a person's brain is at the highest risk for being violent, aggressive, and making poor decisions.[3]

Known risk factors for gang activity include:
- Aggressiveness
- Early initiation of violent behavior
- Parental criminality
- Child maltreatment
- Low levels of parental involvement
- Parent-child separation
- Academic failure
- Lack of school connectedness
- Truancy and school dropout
- Frequent school transitions
- Delinquent siblings and peers
- Peer gang membership
- Poverty
- Substance use (e.g. illicit drugs and alcohol)
- Community disorganization
- Availability of drugs and firearms
- Exposure to violence and racial prejudice[4]

When there is a parent missing in the home, the risk of poverty, drug and alcohol use, dropping out of school, childhood psychopathy, suicide attempts, anger and aggression, and crime increases.[5] For the most part, it is not adults who join gangs. It is people with undeveloped brains who are unsupported at home.

Locking young people away in a non-rehabilitative environment and stripping them of future opportunities does more harm than good. We cannot continue to give up on people because of their past. I have known people who were in gangs and left. One high school friend in particular did horrible things to gain initiation as a teenager. He left the gang in his teens and now has a good job and a beautiful family. People often acknowledge our ability to change, to adapt, but there is a rigidity in our society when it comes to people doing things we feel we would never do such as belonging to a violent gang. It is in our nature to think this way. If a crime is too scary or unimaginable, it becomes easy to discredit a person's humanity because of their behavior. But judging people and pushing them away only causes more people to do things like join gangs and feel that they can't get out. They end up feeling there is no place for them in society. Most likely, they have felt this lack of belonging their entire life growing up without a father or in an underprivileged home. I know I felt this way as a child. If I had easier access to gang membership as a teenager, I know for certain I would have joined a gang, though people who meet me today can never tell I had this kind of life.

Many people who are incarcerated today grew up with an absent parent. Their incarceration means their children now have an absent parent as well. One of the saddest things about our non-rehabilitative prison system is the children it impacts. There are 2.7 million children with parents behind bars who, due to lack of rehabilitation, have a good chance of ending up behind bars again. 1 in every 28 kids in the United States are in this situation. Two thirds of these children's parents are in prison for a non-violent offense.[6]

On top of the grief, loss, and utter desperation children feel when one of their parents is incarcerated, they are often displaced, particularly because most of these children already come from underprivileged households. Often, after a parent is incarcerated, circumstances become much worse for the child. The continuation of this cycle is said to be one of the most catastrophic components of America's justice system.

Without the tools and support to overcome crippling abandonment and loss fatherless children feel, we cannot expect them to function appropriately in society. Still, from writing my pen pals, I know it is not too late. The fatherless child still lies within all of these men, longing for love, longing to be healed, and longing to be a present father for their children.

A BOY WITHOUT A SOUL

Bailey,

A child without their parents is like a puppy without its mother. It grows only to know whoever takes care of it. So a boy without his father is a boy without a soul. All he knows is what the streets taught him. I was once told that I am a strong young man. But that's not true, Bailey. That's only what they see in me. What they don't know won't hurt me. I never had trust in nobody, and I always think negative because that's all I know and that's all I have been around.

I was raised by all women, 2 sisters, a mother and grandmother. No father figure. So treating a female good has always been easy to me. I am overprotective about my little family. What I am saying, Bailey, is no one never taught me how to be a man. I taught myself the in's and out's. Meaning I taught myself how to fight, drive, read, and how to stay alive. All my life I been in the real world. To pin point where I'm coming from is everybody needs a dad. Girls need us as man and father because they need a protector, and boys need us as man and father because we're whose steps they follow.

So without us they will always be ate up by the streets and led by wrongs. I want you to remember this. You never get what you don't ask for, and me as a young man, I never ask for help or a friend. But I am asking you to stay blessed and continue being the best mother you can be. I am always going to be here for you as of now and forever, okay?

To my new and first friend ever. I am gonna end this short story because I got to go get a check up for my bullet wounds. It's been messing with my leg and back. Have a blessed and beautiful day, Bailey.

Andres

THE FOUNDATION

Yo you,

What's up, Bailey! How are you? I hope that when this letter reaches you it finds you and your family in the best of spirits. As for me, maintaining while fighting this battle I'm faced with! Beyond such, I just received your letter. To answer your question, my first son passed away due to heart failure at birth. I'm 28 yrs old, just made 28 in April on the 18th. I like to read James Patterson books and business books because that's something I would like to get into when I touch, and any books I can learn from. I also like to play chess. What do I wish I knew when I was younger? Good question. I wish I would have known that I was the foundation of my family and the things I was into affected them. How my brothers and cousin looked up to me. Maybe things would be different. I'm from the westside of Chicago, grew up in the Rockwell projects. At the age of three I seen people get killed right in front of me, drugs, etc . . . My plan when I touch is to be a father to my son and my brother's two kids. He was shot 24 times in the streets. And I'm going to work on getting my own business! Thank you for the time you take out of your busy day to write me!!!

Booda (Eli Barnes)

SLOW DOWN AND LISTEN

Hey Bailey,

It's good to hear from you. I was scared I ran you off with all of my questions. Like who is this stranger to be asking you all those questions, right? Parole didn't work in my favor. I received a one year set off, so I'll come back up in eight months to see them again. It's a small thing to a giant. I've done the hard part. Everything now is downhill. It just gives me more time to work on me.

I must have stained your brain when I spoke of libraries and liquor stores. I mean if you chose to go that route and open a library in the hood, low-income neighborhood, it would make more of an impact then you think.

Seems like you have some young adults on your hands. You made a statement about foster kids saying you would "like to take in more." Are you saying some of yours are adopted?

I have a son. He's 5 now. I've never met him. Not by choice but by force being incarcerated. At the same time, his mom is not considerate enough to bring him around. What would you do? My mom just made it through breast cancer. She took a loss of one. My dad, I love the old man. He's always been around. He's a good provider, we just never really had too many of those father, son conversations. I mean, I know I played a role with that, not wanting to slow down and listen. I got a son, nieces, nephews, sister and brother, moma, daddy. They all need help, and I feel like I'm the chosen one, so I'm gone keep on striving by all means. With that being said, I'm not all sure of how I'm going to go about it. I don't know Bailey. I just don't like lying to myself saying what I won't do. The fact of the matter is I'm a felon, so I don't know how hard it'll be for me to get a good paying job. I'm not living check to check. If you have some advice, I'd love to hear it.

Nathaniel Townsend

I'M JUST A YOUNG MAN

Hey Ms. Bailey,

How are you doing? You asked me about my plans. I can say what I want to do, but actions speak louder than words. Don't get me wrong. I'm dream chasing, and I know I'm gonna reach my goals. I'm fighting for my life right now. I'm trying to get back into court, so I can get my time fixed. That's my first goal. My second goal is to get home and take care of my loved ones. They need me. Also, you wanted to know more about me. I'm just a young man that's been led wrong all my life. Let's just say I've been in the streets since I was 10 years old, so the streets have always been a home to me. Because I had no father at home, it made me strong being in the streets. I've basically raised myself. "The hard knocks of life was so frequent" . . . that they began to feel like love taps and the traps of the streets was nothing but an obstacle to see who could survive the longest. I've taught myself the ins and outs. You can put yourself in my shoes for one moment, just make sure you give me my Nike's back!

Take care, friend.
Andres

LOOK TO THE STREETS

Hello Bailey,

I am happy to be able to write you and share my story. I'm in the penitentiary for 2 armed robberies and aggravated assault with a deadly weapon. This last time I was out, I was beyond reckless. I was living so fast I hardly thought twice before I acted. I feel like I needed this time to re-evaluate myself and sharpen myself up mentally and physically. I am 2 years into a 7-year sentence. Since birth, I grew up in and out of group homes. Both of my parents were drug addicts, and my dad was physically abusive towards me and my mom, so my mom left my dad when I was young. I grew up without a father and that caused me to look to the streets. When I turned 12, I started taking back and forth trips to juvenile detentions and various institutions. I've had a lot of struggles in my life, but I'm a resilient individual, and I know I will bounce back from anything life throws at me. I pride myself in that. I dropped out of school 2 weeks into freshman year. Most of my education came from juvie. I earned my GED when I was 16. School didn't teach me how to cope with what I was going through at home. But I actually look forward to hearing back from you and hearing your thoughts. I hope life treats you good and sends you blessings.

Sincerely,
Monty Alamos

I CAN SPEAK FOR ME

Hey Bailey,

I really can't speak for all fathers or dads, but I can speak for me. I became absent 2 yrs ago when I came to jail, but I never once thought I would be leaving my kids and coming to jail. I did a lot in the streets but never once thought I would be locked up, and to answer your question, I lack on my kids, and it hurt, so I try to see them twice a month. I always promise myself that I will always be with my kids right or wrong. I never had a father so being in my kids' life means the world to me. To be honest, being in kids' lives period means something to me. I never had a father figure so that's why I love all kids.

Bailey, you said guys in prison never had fathers and the cycle keeps repeating. Out of % it's 95% of guys in here don't have a father. Once again, Bailey, I don't speak for everyone, but my dad got killed! Livin the life I am living. But it's crazy because my dad's mother and my grandmother always tell me to try and break the cycle that my grandad and dad was livin. They both died the same way in the streets. Bailey, that's crazy right? You asked me why did I get shot? I got shot because of the life that I was livin and it's real crazy because I got shot 3 different times in 2015 summer being in the wrong places. Also you asked me how could my teacher have helped me. If they would have taught me and not give up on me maybe I wouldn't be in prison. But I'm not gonna act like I was a good boy, Bailey. I'm not going to lie. I was a problem, and they just couldn't control me. I didn't get along with nobody if they wasn't from my black neighborhood. That's how it was growing up where I'm from in Chicago. Stay blessed, and I will keep you and your family in my heart.

Truly your Andres

A BUM OR A FAILURE

Hey Bailey,

It's good that your daughter is learning ballet at a young age, ballet is both fun and ridiculously hard. As far as I know my sister is taking online business classes. My brother is doing video game design, and my youngest sister is going for music business.

I don't think I'm going to go back to school. If I do it would also be for music business. While I'm here I think I might take the paralegal course, it's a 500 dollar course, and I'll pay 30 a month. I'm hoping I'll learn enough to get out of here.

I still don't know who I want to be, but I know who I don't want to be. I don't want to be a bum or a failure. I don't want to be my Dad or any of my uncles. So pretty much any males in my family. I don't want to be what society expects me to be because of my circumstances. I'm still figuring myself out.

What about you, who do you want to be? And I've been meaning to ask, how did you get into writing?

Your friend
Dale Walker

IF I DID EVERYTHING RIGHT

Bailey,

Thanks so much for writing me back. You said that you was curious to know what programs I thought would help prevent me from going down the path I traveled upon, that led me to where I am today? Well to answer that question, I believe there are many different things that could of helped me when I was younger. First off, I was always a trouble maker, getting into fights, being defiant and using strong profanity. The school I went to just thought I had behavior issues (which they was right). But all they wanted to do was punish me to correct the behavior. Nothing they did worked and the behavior continued. That's because they never tried to look into the root of my issues until it was far too late.

Around 3rd grade I got taken into state custody because of abuse and neglect that was going on in my home. For two long years I bounced around several group homes and foster homes until my father finally got his shit together and got custody of me back. By then, I was mentally fucked up and had a lot of issues. Behavior issues that is. Around 6th or 7th grade my father got diagnosed with cancer. So I tried to be the best son I could be. I was quarterback of the football team, went to boy scouts, and even went to church every weekend with a neighbor. I had to do everything on my own, from making dinner to finding rides to games. For some reason, I thought that if I did everything right, I could prevent my father from dying.

One day I came home from school, and my father could not stop crying. He told me the chemo didn't work and that the doctors told him to have his affairs in order before Christmas. To say the least I didn't take that shit too good at 13. My dad started a second round of chemo, but I already lost all hope. I started skipping school and doing drugs. As soon as I started getting high, I lost all feelings and emotions and began down a path of self-destruction. The second round of chemo my dad took helped him but was nowhere near making him healthy. The trouble I was getting into started bringing a lot of attention, especially because I lived in a small town. So we moved to Florida, where I ended up in rehabs and jail.

I'm sorry for going on and on about my life. Anyways, programs I believe would be good that could of helped me growing up are probably something to do with the grieving process. Also maybe some classes on cognitive thinking. I can't help but think that if there was more educational support when I was younger, it might of played a part in whether I would or wouldn't be where I am today. But to be honest I wouldn't change my circumstances because everything I been through in life has shaped me into the great man that I am today. I just hope that others don't have to follow in my footsteps. I'm a little curious to know what hard times you had growing up. I really appreciate you for writing and communicating with me.

Thank you for our time
Abram

PREVAIL

Today I feel down lonely and my facial expression
Just seems to be stuck in a frown
How else to feel when thinking about death?
But no, you misconstrue my sentiments
I think about the lives that could've been

The lives that never were but should've been
These lives I speak of are my miscarried offspring
I wish so bad to be a father but why?
Is it because I never had one?

Is it because I'm a product of rape

Or just that I know I'll be the opposite of a bad one?
I don't know, only time will tell
Whether or not I get released from prison
And continue to fail
Maybe I'll get a record deal and make an effort to excel
I hope I'll do well
I will prevail

By Abraham Johnson

MY PLAN

Hey Bailey!

I'm 24 years old, born and raised on the Southside of Chicago. I dropped out when I was a junior. What made me drop out was I was in the streets, and I had got shot up so at that time, I wasn't in school anymore. Then when I healed up, I just stopped going. I wish I would have learned more about school than the streets because it took me somewhere that I didn't want to be. Also, you asked me why I'm locked up. Because of guns, money, and drugs. Bailey, see where I'm from most of my homies never had a father or a father figure so the bad was always good to use. My plan is to help kids out and to talk and tell them not to follow the same path I went down.

Stay blessed and safe.

From: Andres Dixon

LOOKIN FOR LOVE

Bailey,

How are you doing today? Did you get that one letter when I said I see you write a lot of people? I seen a photo of you on someone else's photos, and I was like oh she write you too, bro? And he said yeah and you have kids and a wife. So I was like where did you write her, and he said "friends behind the wall." Yeah, it's like three of us as your penpal here.

Well, I've been in prison since I was 15 years old. This is my first time, but this prison system is f-word up and people try to start things to get time off and paid. By getting hurt by inmates. I want to get a job, learn how to not come here or back.

The big thing I see is mental health. I was 18 years old when I heard a man get killed in the cell not too far from me, and I thought to myself I'm in a max security with 7 years and all the other inmates have life or life+ 60 years to do. Nothing to lose in their eyes. So the officers are told to act or do things, ways a lifer inmate is supposed be treated. The facility are supposed to fix the people and get them back on the road of opportunity to succeed in life. All I'm learning is to do more B.S. or get worse. There is no help being given here, no.

I was lookin for love from a brother or father type, and I got love from gangbanging. The streets was my father, and my mother was my mother.

Well I heard from my babys mother. She wrote me, and we miss one another. But in time I'll be back with her and family soon.

Thank you for being my friend and giving me your time as well. God bless you and family.

Take care. Hugs!
Romeo Grant

P.S. I'm just trying to get home safe and show people like me or who are going down the road of gangs or whatever that's bad, man. It is not worth it! Hell is really real, and where I come from, that's what it is.

AN ALTERNATE UNIVERSE

Bailey,

I wrote you a quick note around the 10th or so of last month telling you of a situation I had gotten myself into. It has resulted in my losing the job I had, being moved from the program I was enrolled in as well as being moved to the other side of the prison, a more restrictive area where my movements are more controlled. It will be like this for a minimum of 6 months and a maximum of 12 months. During that time, no job, confined to the cell 20 to 22 hours a day. Every day.

The worst part was that I lost the job. It brought me in contact with guys who were in the very situation I find myself in now! People who need encouragement. Guys who need answers to serious questions about being a man, about building a life after prison, about how to process all the negative information we are bombarded with in this place. Anti-America, Anti-White, Anti-Europe, Anti-Christian, Anti-Mortality, anti everything.

They have no sense of historical context, no idea of the components of "facts," "evidence," "proof" or "truth." They are actually being militarized against their fellow Americans! Just consider the group held at Guantanamo Bay in Cuba. All weren't guilty, but even so they can't be released. Because while held there they've been radicalized by the "real" bad guys. They may have undergone "enhanced interrogation" just to determine that they weren't a terrorist, but the process of determining that they weren't a terrorist has left them with a very bad taste in their mouth about America. And the real bad guys exploit this fast. THIS is why we can't let them go. Even if our enemies will use their bitterness and negative experience to recruit others and our leaders understand that.

It's the same thing that's happening in prisons across America and the west. People outside our country and inside are using this negative prison experience to turn prisoners against America and the west. And guys are walking out the front door of this place just as "radicalized" and indoctrinated and screwed up as the people held in Guantanamo Bay Prison. And they've been influenced by the very same people, Bailey.

Bailey, this is an alternate universe in this place. There is literally a battle for the hearts and minds of these young men. Inside and outside this place.

My purpose is to tell this story. #1 to counter the influence of these recruiters inside this place. #2 to expose the lie so often used to recruit #3 and really wake America up to the process of recruitment in prison and the streets of these young men. If there is to be some type of prison reform THAT should be at the epicenter of it.

What do you believe is your purpose? I didn't find mine (or what I believe to be mine) until I was 40+ years old.

What motivates you? I mean the help others bent when most your age won't get a "help others" bent until much later in their lives if ever. I look at your pictures and I question you Bailey. A young attractive woman reaching out to me in this darkness. Where did you come from? You have someone you love and have committed yourself to. You have a home full of laughing children. You're healthy, you're smart, and I needed someone just like you, Bailey. A person like you should have turned their attention inward. But you've done that but at the same time left room in your heart for someone like me and the other misfits that you correspond with. I want you to know that this is not lost on me, Bailey.

I need you. I respect you. I accept you. I appreciate you. I admire you. I'm grateful to you. I am thankful for you. And anything and everything else that I may have overlooked.

You came along at a very important time in my life and a defining point in the unfolding of my purpose. And any help you can be in that will be truly appreciated.

I am going to close now. My best wishes go out to you and your family, and I ask that whenever you send up a prayer, mention this old guy.

Floyd Ike Williams

GOD IS ALSO MISUNDERSTOOD

Dear Bailey,

Well, where would I go when I'm out? To the women that's been there since it all happened. To my mothers house to get myself together, and then, only time we tell. I'm 22, just turned! I was only 15 yrs old when I caught my case for 2nd degree murder. After high school? Well, first off a job! At the time, I had a kid that wasn't born yet but died when this case came to me.

I ran to the streets looking for a man. That was needed in my life, and my mother is the one that tried to teach me what a man need to, but she can't. She tried, and I love my mother for that! She's my world! So I started to cut the place off that I like on other men that was around, and that's how I made myself now! But that want on lonely nights, gangbangin for reasons why I sit here writing you.

I know this is not the life for me, but it's a part of me! I paid with my life just looking for that love from a brother, dad, someone! I was in class, and this one girl said to me, "Mario why do you gangbang?" I said "I have some of what I've been looking for! Love!" And so she said "I Love you Romeo!" Well I got a book telling you about me.

I gang-banged, hanged, fought and slang. Did all sorts of crime, start having sexual relations at ten years old. I paid attention in school like I should. I knew I was doing wrong out there, and each day I knew I would. There are many faces, distractions and practices in the hood. All the negativity been no good. Although we was born in the hood, this doesn't have to be our destiny! We to can be successful and rich, righteous and good. We must excel. When things get rough, we must remain focus! We must trust in God because God is good! God has produced billions of winners from the hood. Here's a news flash, God is also from the hood, and God is also misunderstood. When we're from the hood, it's always a constant would, could and should. The hood taught us evil vs. good. I just know we can all do a lot better. You do a lot, my friend, by giving me time to open my mind, and when you send some pics of whatever, I look in the background just to be there with you. That takes me away from this hell hole, and I thank you for that!

Romeo Grant

FACTS ABOUT FATHERLESSNESS

"More than one in four fathers in the United States who have children 18 or younger now lives apart from their children, according to Pew."[7]
—*USA Today*

In 1999, 72.2% of the population said that fatherlessness was the most significant family or social problem facing America.[8]

On the ACES test, 28% of the general population in the United States reports that they grew up with their parents living apart. 70% of incarcerated individuals answered that they grew up with parents living apart. With a difference of 42%, this is one of the biggest gaps we see in ACES between the general and prison population.[9]

1 in 28 children in the United States has a parent behind bars.[10]

DRUGS

Drugs take hold of people and demand control over every part of their lives: finances, relationships, time, spirituality, and purpose. People like my friend, Izaak, "deteriorate to a skeleton." People lose the things that matter most to them. I have seen drug abusers and addicts end up in prison, sometimes for the rest of their lives. Trauma inhibits a person's ability to think cognitively and make healthy decisions, and people with trauma are much more susceptible to drug addiction. And, of course, once someone starts doing drugs, it is very hard to stop.

I came very close to being another person who ended up in prison. I did drugs. I sold drugs. I spent most of my time with people who were burglarizing liquor stores and breaking into people's cars. They all ended up going to jail or prison. Some of them are still there. If I had easier access to drugs then, I would have done more. If I had been recruited to sell more drugs than I already did, I would have.

When we send addicts to prison, drugs are still accessible. Drugs are sometimes just as accessible in prison as they are out of it. Prison isn't rehab, and based on our country's current recidivism rates ("2 out of 3 people are rearrested and more than 50% are reincarcerated"[1]), we can safely assume that these drug arrests are not keeping people from committing crimes after a prison sentence or keeping our country any safer.

Drugs are one of the most important items on the agenda for improving our nation's failing justice system. Conditions are bad, rehabilitation is close to nonexistent, but why are so many people being thrown behind bars in the first place? Our brain is wired to see things in black and white, but that is not the way the world works. To see the truth about the war on drugs and our nation's sentencing laws, we have to open our minds to the possibility that there is more to this story than a person does something bad, so they get punished.

Since the 1980s, there has been an enormous rise in the prison population. We went from having 300,000 people incarcerated in our country in 1980 to over 2 million in the year 2000. The amount of drug arrests that led to prison sentences quadrupled.[2] This significant change in our incarcerated population is, surprisingly, not because of crime rates. Other countries like Germany and Finland with similar crime rates had a prison population that between 1960 and 1990 either stayed the same or decreased while ours skyrocketed. Governments decide on disciplinary policies, which depend mainly on how much they want to punish. Our incarceration rates, which are six to ten times higher than other industrialized nations, show that punishment is not driven by crime.[3] Punishment is driven by fear. The enormous rise in incarceration can be traced back to the war on drugs, a set of drug policies spearheaded by the United States during the Nixon presidency.

While I cannot speak to the intentions of those who founded the policy, it quickly became a racist one. Once more, blacks and other minorities found themselves in a system of social control. Slavery turned into segregation and segregation into incarceration. Every bit of evidence points to the need for drugs to become more of a public health problem. Yet, we continue to heavily incarcerate people for drug crimes.

Though the war on drugs started before crack was introduced in the late 1980s, as soon as crack became popular, the opportunity to feature black people doing drugs was capitalized on. Photos of black people strung out on the drug were featured throughout the campaign even though cocaine was just as popular. There are no pharmacological differences between crack and cocaine, but you wouldn't know this based on the sentencing. There is a 100-1 ratio where "just 5 grams of crack carries a minimum 5-year federal prison sentence, while distribution of 500 grams of powder cocaine carries the same 5-year mandatory minimum sentence."[4]

People do not like to think about addicts because it triggers disgust. When something seems dirty, we push it away, and sometimes we even criminalize it.

We like to think of ourselves as rational. We all believe that we are able to look at a situation, review the evidence, and make a reasonable conclusion, but nearly everything we do is based on our instincts and a story we tell ourselves.

In his book *Unfair: The New Science of Criminal Justice*, Adam Benforado details the following account. A couple, outside their home in a safe and wealthy neighborhood, found a man lying on the grass. He was semi-conscious and having a difficult time speaking or sitting up. The couple called the police, and a group of firefighters arrived at the scene. The unconscious man had thrown up, and when one of the firefighters got close, he recognized the smell as alcohol. He told the other firefighters it was nothing but a drunk, and they shared the diagnosis with the paramedics once they arrived.

At the hospital, the man was placed on a gurney in the hallway for hours before he was given an exam because everyone thought the man was just another passed out drunk. It was not until his exam hours after he had been sitting in a hallway gurney that the nurse noticed a contradiction with the story provided. Abdominal distention was indicative of a brain injury.

Once they figured out that this man, a dedicated and acclaimed New York Times reporter of over 35 years, had a serious brain injury and had actually been attacked, they rushed him into surgery. But it was too late.[5] He passed away based on a few people's overconfidence in their own abilities to be rational and deduce the circumstances using their own mind instead of relying on protocol and completing every necessary procedure. So what was it that caused these trained professionals to make such a profound mistake? Disgust. The extensive studies done on this devastating string of human errors traces the mishap back to the vomit the firefighter first smelled.

Our minds correlate drug addiction with dirtiness. We feel disgusted. Maybe this is why we have such an easy time charging taxpayers billions of dollars to throw addicts behind bars for decades without drug therapy.

Users and addicts are people. They have inherent value, and nothing—no drug, no crime, no prison sentence—can ever take that away.

GATEWAY

Bailey

You've been through a lot of shit. I have a mother that's bipolar, has a mental illness and probably some social disorders as well (lol). My grandparents raised my brother and I. My father was never, not once, a part of my life. Broken dysfunctional family.

My mom was always getting high, selling drugs. After she went to state prison she got a little better. Now she's living like a hippie somewhere in North Carolina. She still writes and sends money here and there. But she lives without an address, so I can't even write her back. I have to send it somewhere else so she'll get it. Complicated.

The first time I was adjudicated (sent away) I was 15 too. I never ran away. I was with my mom, and we were at the creek swimming and fishing (war story lol), and her boyfriend was this alcoholic roofer dude that had an opiate addiction. Well, my mom had a bunch of pills in her purse, and I went to grab a cigarette, and I found them. I was a 15 year old, and I knew methadones when I saw them, so I took a shit ton. I had a tolerance that my mom didn't know about. She thought I just smoked weed. She started freaking out, ended up calling my po. She was on state parole, and she was worried if I OD'd she would get a technical violation. So I got a urine. Failed with flying colors. He told me to sign myself into rehab or we'll go through the court system. I signed myself in, being ignorant of law and that shit. I was in rehab for 3 months. Came home, relapsed, got locked up for a year, came home when I was 17. I was home for like a couple months, became addicted to crystal meth, went crazy, my P.O. locked me up for another year.

I came home, 18, healthy, had my own house. Good job. Alcohol. Weed. Pills. Meth. In that sequence. I completely deteriorated to a skeleton. I lost everything in 3 months. Homeless. That shit wasn't that bad honestly.

Well. Enough of that shit.

From my experience, children such as myself who are/were troubled growing up should be taught their rights. They should know the law because sooner or later in their lives they will be in need of it. If they are not taught, they will become a slave.

Proper psychiatric and therapeutic processes should be instituted. It was hard for me to connect with people I felt were trespassing into my life. Children and youth, I hated them. I couldn't relate to them. How am I supposed to tell somebody that I don't or am unable to trust things that are even hard for me to comprehend or deal with? In certain situations those organizations tend to do more harm than good.

Peer pressure was a definite factor for me. I was always with the wrong people. The "right" people probably would have accepted me, but I didn't like them. They probably didn't like me either. If I had children, I would homeschool them. I wouldn't even let them be tainted by a public school.

Drugs, of any kind, any mind influencing or mood altering substances should be avoided. It was a gateway for me, and probably you—prescription medication. Look up the percentage rates that tell you that an overwhelming proportion of Americans are on antidepressants or shit like that.

I have a lot of respect for your purpose. I will contribute whatever way possible.

Write back soon!

Izaak Shunk

A MAJOR MISTAKE

Bailey

I'm 33, and I went to school in Oklahoma. I was kicked out of school in 9th grade. My English teacher was gonna fail me if I didn't start asking for help and get my grades up, so I tried and was ignored repeatedly until I finally got fed up and said some things to her I really regret. If I could, I would apologize to her, but I don't know her name.

I started going for my GED, and I got mixed up in drugs. My life spiraled out of control. I started running away and cooking meth and living the life of an addict when I was 17. I thought I got a girl pregnant, so I married her, got sober, went to work in the oil field, and was doing good for about two years until I found out she was cheating on me. I was devastated. She then told me when our child was almost three he wasn't mine. I didn't believe her, but she took him and disappeared for years. I didn't know anything. I went into self-destruct mode and got all mixed up on drugs again. For years all I did was run the streets doing drugs. I abandoned my whole family in 2008. I caught a robbery case and landed in prison were I stayed for almost 6 years. Upon my release, I met a woman. I fell deeply in love with her and her kids while I was locked up. We moved in together and things were going really good but with a criminal record and no education, it is really hard to get work or housing, so I turned to the only thing I knew I could do to support us—sell drugs. Worst mistake I have ever made. I had just been locked up for 6 years and after being out for only 14 days I got busted with meth trafficking, which landed me back in prison on the 20-year sentence I'm doing now. I've been back in for four years now.

Since coming back, I have devoted my time to programs, God, and my family. I have completed ABE, Kairos, and a volunteer substance abuse program for the last 6 months. I would tell kids to please take it from me that life isn't always easy and to, no matter what, buckle down and take education seriously. You see, I've lived most of my life as a criminal and a drug addict who always said, huh school? Why? Who needs that? But school is very important. Even though you may think it's cool to go to parties and skip school, it is a major mistake. Devote those little 16 to 18 years to school, get educated, and stay away from drugs and alcohol. Prison is no place for anybody. It's horrible.

I have recently enrolled in International Christian College and Seminary to get my associates degree in counseling. I want to travel and tell my story. Recently, God has answered a lot of my prayers, and I should be out in four or so years with the new law changes. I really wish I had taken school serious and graduated. Without an education, it's hard to get anywhere in life and even harder with a record. Please do what you must to finish school. You have your whole life to try it your way. Growing up, I always thought my parents and family and teachers were telling me stuff because it's what they wanted, but really they were telling me the things they were saying because they loved me and didn't want to see me struggle. The effects of not listening were the complete ruin of my life. Had I listened, I would be educated and have my own business now, living the good life. Not staring at razor wire everyday. I am a really good guy, just made bad decisions I am trying to correct. Thank you and best wishes.

Sincerely,
Jerum Landing

THE SIMPLE THINGS IN LIFE

Hey Bailey,

I agree with you on the view that everyone deserves a fighting chance to be successful. The other aspect of that is that some are given opportunities to succeed but squander them. I believe myself to fall into that category. I really did care for math but didn't see a need for it. I figured as long as I could count money, I was good. I should have paid a little more attention. Perhaps I wouldn't be here. My plan after high school was to get a decent job, get married, and take care of my family. Things just didn't work out that way. I did get a fairly good job doing logging work, but it is damn dangerous work. I was making $11.50/hour, but I was working 40 to 60 hours a week. Working like that and never getting ahead is what started me down the road to crime. I got tired of working my ass off and barely keeping my head above water.

So knowing people on the seedy side of life I got hooked up and started to buy stolen guns and stolen cars. I was turning a good profit. Then I got into doing meth and that stuff makes you feel invincible. I ended up going on the run from charges from the guns and cars. So I was losing money and my mind. So I ended up robbing a store. Those things combined are what landed me here in prison. That isn't the person I truly am or want to be. I'm trying to use this time to get my life together and become a better person, so that I can get out and do what I intended all along, and that is to take care of my children and family. I've learned to be happy with the simple things in life and not live outside my means. I hope this gives you a little insight to who I am. I hope to hear from you soon.

Adam Condor

THE CHOICES THAT YOU MAKE

Bailey

Well I'll tell you a little bit about myself. I am 21 years old. I am from a small school and played football, and I was really good at it. It inspired me to keep going. But the downfall of my high school was that I really struggled with my grades. And I tried my hardest to make the time to study and go work construction. But the hardest thing about my high school is that I am half Mexican, and everyone else was all white. Most people were hateful, including most teachers. I felt the teachers wouldn't give me the extra help I needed in my studies. So I was angry and lost hope, and I dropped out as a junior. I wish I would have learned at an early age to be patient in life and that being angry doesn't have to control the choices that you make. But after I dropped out of school my life went downhill from there. I was working 12 hour days with my brothers and, of course, like brothers, we were always arguing and fighting. So I went on doing work for people, but I was by myself so I couldn't do a lot of big jobs. And I wasn't making as much money. That's when I started to sell drugs.

Everything was good. I'm helping my mother pay her bills, and I finally got arrested for possession of heroin. When I was in jail, the judge let me out on work release. I was trying to work my fastest, and I was an hour late returning back to jail. They charged me with escape. I was so mad and disappointed in myself. So they sentenced me to 5 years for possession and escape. I am thankful I don't have any kids right now because it would be much harder on me and them. So for that I am blessed.

If the public was in my hands, I would try my hardest to change the hate and the racism that we struggle with today. And I wish schools taught life's real challenges like death, relationships, natural disasters, and how to make the world a better/safer place for our children. Well, Bailey, I want to thank you for the time you're taking to hear about my story. I hope you won't look at me any different because I'm locked up for selling drugs.

*Your friend,
Reese Mendez*

KICKING MYSELF IN THE ASS

Hello Bailey,

I'm currently 23 years old. So I've lived on a ranch for 6 years in Arizona. I've been riding and working with horses since I was two years old. My family have been involved with horses their whole life. My mom's side of the family. My dad is a city slicker. I have 5 sisters and no brothers. I've roped cattle and bulls most of my life. I'm in prison because at the age of 18, I started doing drugs and committed felonies.

I've worked on vehicles most of my life as well. I am successful in the automotive sector and ranch life. I'm a social butterfly with certain people. Smaller the circle, colder the beer I like to say. I am currently attempting to further my future in firefighting and diesel mechanics. Im kicking myself in the ass everyday for not becoming what I've always wanted to be. My dad is a 18-year fireman paramedic, and I've always wanted to become that.

I'm a redneck. I love Copenhagen, Coors light, Dodge Cumming diesels, Chevy Duramaxes, intelligent women, family gatherings, hunting, fishing, roping, and being in small towns where I don't have to affiliate or waste my life with city slickers and dumbasses.

James Maple

I WOULD NEVER BREAK YOUR HEART

Hey Bay Bay,

I guess I got my hopes up a little too high on getting out sooner than expected. It turns out my charges don't qualify for the new senate bill. It really saddens me. I really wanted to surprise my babies. I wasn't even gonna tell them. There's been some stupid things going on here. There are a lot of drugs on the yard. One of my buddies I found out is strung out. He knows I hate drugs and had the nerve to ask me if I wanted to get high. I told him what kind of stupid question is that. I told him he knows better than to disrespect me with a stupid f'n question like that. Yes, I cussed at him. Please forgive me for that. A youngster heard me and asked why I wont get high? I actually pointed at your pic. I told him you are the only person I have and I would never let you down or break your heart. Three days later my buddy hadn't slept. He said he thinks everybody is trying to jump him. I told him I wouldn't allow that. I told him he was tripping and told him to go to sleep. When I went back to my building, next thing I know everybody told me he freaked out and the cops took him and about five others that freaked out. There are very few of us who don't get high. They drug tested 10 guys, only one passed. Crazy, huh?

I'm on the right path, but this is still prison. Only the strong survive in here. This is a cruel place. You gotta realize there are dudes in here for murder, doing life, and they will survive by any means necessary. Those of us that have done time for a long time know the game, and we will do the same if our backs are against the wall. None of this drama involves me, so I'm gonna lay in my cell until all of this unfolds. Because I have an angel out there I want to meet when I get out. I'm not giving that up for nobody. I'm your biggest fan, and you are my gift from god.

Jason

I WANTED TO GIVE MY SON EVERYTHING

Hey,

I decided to write you and answer some of your questions. I am 26 years old and I, as well, have kids. Well only a son. He is 7 years old. I'm here for selling heroin because I always wanted to give my son everything. Right after school I went to ISU because my dream job is to be a preschool/kindergarten teacher. After my jail sentence, I will go back to school part time and work part time. I do hope to hear from you again. Letters are always a welcome thing.

Sincerely,
Russ Thompson

KNUCKLEHEADS ON THE YARD

Hey Bay Bay,

I just got your letter. Thank you for writing me. I kinda needed something to cheer me up a bit. Yeah it's been a little crazy here. The good news is they finally caught the guy bringing most of the drugs on the yard. They caught him bringing it in through visitation. But there is never just one person bringing it in. I'd say at least 65%-75% of people in prison use drugs. They bring in all drugs: meth, heroin, weed, spice, saboxon strips, fetenal (phetenol), you name it. It's just as easy to get in here as it is on the streets. Thank you for the respect on not using. I work very hard on my sobriety.

I overheard a guy talking about how this kid had really bad smelly feet that was stinking up the whole dorm in another building, and a lot of people were kinda making fun of him. I asked the guy who the kid was, and it was one of my youngsters. I know the kid has no help with money from the streets, so I bought him a brand new pair of sneakers and gave him a few pairs of my new socks too. I'm really big on hygiene, especially in here. It's so nasty. 75% of the inmate population has Hep C. Plus people catch mrsa and staph. I'm really big about taking care of my feet. I have very beautiful feet. Lol. My feet are very well taken care of.

I only talk to you, my dad, and my stepmom. My sister fell off again. I read my truck magazines. Lol. I don't have any books except the one you sent me. I loaned it out to a guy, and he gave it back yesterday. 90% of these guys aren't ready for that kind of change in their life. I'm still not working. I just hustle around the yard to make money: making brownies, tattoos, running a little commissary store. I did send $650 home to my stepmom this last month to save for a truck for work. I have $1,100 saved up. I sell food boxes for $100.00. I *give them $80.00 in food, and they send my mom the money.*

I finally got the tattoo with your name drawn up. It says Bailey with little stars around it. I think you will like it. It's not a big tattoo. It's kinda small. But it is gonna hurt very badly. Lol. The ribs are no joke.

Today is my 38th B-Day. I hope today goes as well as I can expect it too. I'm hoping we can cook something today. I am a master microwave chef by the way. I'm hoping I might get a b-day card from my babies. I don't wanna get my hopes too high though. My dad said I'd be lucky if my son's mom will even give him my letter I sent for his b-day. My family doesn't like my kids' mom. My dad said she looked pretty messed up the last time he saw her. I don't know if she's using or not. I really hope she's not.

Some guys in here have been acting like fools. Someone got jumped, and a few of the knuckle heads on the yard got run off. The guy who got jumped actually came back and started raising hell. Now, we are on lockdown today because the cops are worried we might have a riot. Which word travels fast in here so there could be a riot with maybe some California guys. They've been bullying people and stealing. The whole yard is fed up with the problems these guys have been causing. I just chill out of the mix, but everyone tries to involve me. I just tell them I ain't running any yards anymore, so don't involve me. That's the whole reason I'm in this yard. I ran the last yard at catalina. I was what they called the head or the spokesperson of all the white boys on the yard. Prison is very political as far as race goes, but over the last year we have integrated, so I stepped out of the political game, but this new yard is all clicks. I don't have a click. I do me, and that's it. Things might get dangerous the next few days. The tension on the yard is thick. I don't get involved in the drama. If I feel I have to protect myself, I will. What's crazy about a prison riot is it's everybody against everybody. If you're in the wrong place at the wrong time, you could be a victim even if you're not involved.

8-27 (different ink)
Sorry it's been really crazy here. I lost track of the letter for a few days. We almost had a riot a few days ago. The whole yard ran the guys causing problems on the yard off. Then the other night, I just got out of the shower and something happened where a guy in our pod stole some stuff, so about 12 guys in my dorm stomped him out. I'm surprised he didn't get air vac'd. It's been really crazy. Then our commissary has been screwed up for two weeks. Nobody got store, so that's a big problem too. I'm officially under a year now on Aug 22.

Yours always,
Jason

THE LIFE I HAVE LEFT

Bailey

Well, let me start by saying thanks for the return letter. I don't get much mail. As for getting clean and staying clean, it has been a battle, but it feels amazing, and I really owe it to my family too. They are great. Well, what's left of them. I'm just an addict in recovery trying to right my wrongs and make something of the life I have left. You see, I am currently taking courses to become a Christian counselor. I guess in a way we are both on a mission to change something—me with kids, teens, and young adults with addiction and family problems. You see there isn't a lot I haven't been through, and I really know how to connect with people. I don't wanna make a sob of it. I will be working full time in the oil field, but on my days off I will devote a lot of my free time volunteering different places, telling my story and lending a hand in whatever way I can. It is always a joy to hear from you. Until next time, know you are appreciated and valued.

Your friend,
Jerum Landing

FACTS ABOUT DRUGS

We went from having 300,000 people incarcerated in our country in 1980 to over 2 million in the year 2000. The amount of drug arrests that led to prison sentences quadrupled.[6]

Policy changes during the war on drugs have been said to make up for the *entire* increase in the prison population for the twenty years after 1980 when the war on drugs really started to take effect.[7]

Current federal drug sentencing guidelines can impose a five-year mandatory minimum for possession alone.[8]

SENTENCING

For years, I have been receiving letters that prove every statistic regarding the mistreatment that happens during the sentencing process. This may be the most important section of this book. Our criminal justice system is racist. It is also massive and encompasses many variables, but the injustice happening today is not due to mistakes bound to happen in a large criminal justice system. It is not a slight blunder. The criminal justice system has become a system of social control in the United States. These are not radical opinions. They are facts. Everything I share here, I discovered over the last year I spent diving into books and academic journals. Please, don't just take it from me. Go to the real professionals. I especially recommend *The New Jim Crow* by Michelle Alexander. I am an avid reader, having read more than a book/week for most of my life, and I believe *The New Jim Crow* is one of the most important books published in the last 100 years. A lot of the information I cite came from Michelle Alexander's research.

The Fourth Amendment of the constitution is being regularly ignored. Most people do not even know what it says. The Fourth Amendment clearly states our nation shall not conduct unreasonable search and seizure. Yet, this is something we consistently practice because of a small and overly abused loophole. If an officer asks you for the right to search and you grant permission, the officer can legally search your property and use incriminating evidence against you.[1]

We are not educated on criminal justice in school or how to avoid unnecessary trouble, something my pen pals have shared to be a colossal detriment to their lives. There is already a fear of police, especially in minority communities that are over-searched and over-incarcerated.

It is unlikely that someone like me, a seemingly put together white woman in a minivan full of children, would be searched or, say, an elderly white woman. It would be unthinkable for an officer to even ask unless seriously prompted to do so. But for a young, minority male, the likelihood is high. Young black men are a target.[2] Of course, if there is no warrant, we have the right to refuse. But if you don't know this and a police officer, someone with authority who you are already afraid of, asks to search your vehicle, of course you would step out and allow the search. If I were in that position, I know it would be hard to see any other option.

If these illegal searches and seizures were conducted regularly in middle-class white neighborhoods, there would be public outrage. *All* of the wrongs committed against minorities in the criminal justice system would come to an abrupt halt if they were equally committed against whites. But they're not.

We could say, just don't do anything suspicious. Don't break the law, and you will be fine. But people break the law in minor ways all the time. Not stopping the exact amount of time before a light, following just slightly too close behind a vehicle, j-walking, or driving a couple miles an hour above the speed limit could be used to justify a pull over—small offenses we see dozens of times every day. And if there is a subconscious bias at play, it doesn't really matter what you do. It is very possible that, at some point, an officer might stop you. That is one of the reasons parents of black children feel it necessary to have conversations with their kids telling them not to wear hoods, to avoid walking around at night, and to practice great caution when it comes to police. "The talk" has been going on for generations, and by necessity, it continues today among black communities.

Unreasonable search and seizure is so common now that it barely matters what the constitution says. It is happening. I am not against the police by any means. They are a vital part of our society. I have friends who are police officers, and I am grateful for the important work they do. But there is a bias happening everywhere, and when it happens in the criminal justice system as it is now, the results destroy lives, communities, and in my opinion, this bias in the criminal justice system is eating away at our country. America is supposed to be a symbol of freedom. Stripping a person of their freedom and their life because of their race is not the American way.

Even when a search and seizure is not unreasonable—that is, it is warranted because there is legitimate proof of a reason to search a home or vehicle—after the war on drugs, these searches have become unreasonable in their own way.

Excessive force is commonly used for drug crimes. And not just for major drug lords selling huge amounts of narcotics. We are talking about minor drug offenses with searches yielding as little as a few grams of cocaine or marijuana.[3] These unforeseen and forced military-style police raids cause a lot of damage and trauma to the people involved. Sometimes, it may seem unavoidable and justifiable like in the situation of a criminal known to be dangerous. But these raids are happening with non-violent criminals who are only potential sellers of a small amount of drugs. SWAT teams might throw grenades and point guns at everyone in the home including young children. Innocent people, including elderly and underage family members, are being killed in mishandled raids. Again, if an incident like this happened in an affluent white neighborhood, I believe the public would be outraged, and these incidents would quickly be put to a stop. But they are happening in low-income minority neighborhoods, so raids like this continue.[4] Justice Thurgood Marshall, in response to unreasonable search and seizures, felt the need to remind his coworkers about the Fourth Amendment, stating there is no "drug exception."[5]

Forceful and traumatic drug raids are unjust. But the saddest part about the war on drugs is people losing huge portions of their life to imprisonment for minor drug crimes. Most people would look at our incarceration rates in America and assume the explosion in the prison population was a result of our crime rates. They would be wrong. Sentencing laws are becoming recognized as cruel. Changes in policy during the war on drugs have been said to make up for the *entire* increase in the prison population for the twenty years after 1980 when the war on drugs really started to take effect.[6] Judges have been quietly protesting unfair sentencing laws by refusing to take on drug cases like Judge Jack Weinstein who said sending people away because of the war on drugs caused him to feel a sense of depression.[7] Judge Stanely Marshall said, "I've always been considered a fairly harsh sentencer, but it's killing me that I'm sending so many low-level offenders away for all this time." [8] Judges are even going so far as to quit because they are the ones who have to enforce the laws policy makers create. These same people who went to school to promote justice and equity are the ones who must act out our nation's policies and see lives ruined by iniquity.[9] A *New York Times* article quoted Judge Lawrence Irving when speaking about his retirement. "If I remain on the bench," he said, "I have no choice but to follow the law. I just can't, in good conscience, continue to do this." [10]

The war on drugs has not reduced drug use or drug-related crime. Research has proven the ineffectiveness and tragic consequences of the war on drugs. This is not a war on drugs, after all. It is a war on race.

I started to notice a pattern in high school. My white friends, no matter what they did, never seemed to get in trouble. They came to school high on cocaine. We even did drugs in the school parking lot. They consistently drove drunk, sometimes without license plates on their car. There were two white boys at my school who sold more drugs than anyone I knew. Yet, these people were never arrested. They never even got a misdemeanor or any serious repercussions for their reckless behavior unless they did something outrageously stupid like one of my acquaintances who brought a gun to a children's park and showed it off to his friends. The gun had been stolen from a liquor store he burglarized the night before. This boy served only a couple months in prison.

Friends of mine who were Black, Hispanic, and Native American had to be a lot more careful. They went off campus to do drugs and drink. None of them owned cars, so they didn't have a chance to drive drunk or be reckless with a vehicle. None of these friends sold drugs regularly. Yet, every single one of them was arrested while we were in high school together. Every single one. If they didn't show up to school one day, we knew they were locked up. One of these friends is in prison today as a repeat offender. I know for a fact that a couple of my white friends are still doing drugs and being reckless, but I haven't heard of any of them going to jail or prison. In my experience, when one of my white friends does drugs, he goes to rehab. When one of my minority friends does drugs, he goes to prison.

My pen pals sometimes tell me they are grateful for being sent away. Being removed from their situation helped them gain perspective. These conclusions are drawn from a year or two in prison. If you are facing a

20-year sentence, I can't imagine how you would be grateful to have such a large chunk of your life taken away. And in prison, it truly is taken away.

Drug sentencing is particularly outrageous, sending people away with 5-year minimums and 40-year maximums for possession alone (not sales).[11] Not only are these mandatory sentences nonsensical for dealing with crime and drug abuse, but they are also expensive for taxpayers. Mass incarceration cost taxpayers nearly $87 billion in 2015.[12]

The three strikes law is just one example. It imposes harsh punishment for repeat offenders. After three "violent" felonies, you get a life sentence. Initially, the law stemmed from a murder case. Preventing actually violent crimes like murder makes sense, but this is often not how the three strikes law is used. More than half of the offenders being sentenced to life under the three strikes law committed a non-violent crime. Many things about the three strikes law are worth questioning. If you have two felonies from twenty or thirty years prior, you are still subject to this law. You could be living a productive life in society and make one mistake that leads you to a life sentence. Stanford Law School has started a project to help those who, for a nonviolent offense, were given a life sentence under the three strikes law. Stanford wrote about their work, "Project clients have been given life sentences for offenses including stealing one dollar in loose change from a parked car, possessing less than a gram of narcotics, and attempting to break into a soup kitchen." [13]

The Rolling Stones published an article titled "Cruel and Unusual Punishment: While Wall Street Crooks walk, thousands sit in California prisons for life over crimes as trivial as stealing socks." The article tells the story of a man who grew up tough. He had committed a couple of robberies as a kid in the early 1980s but had gotten his life together and been working a good job as a forklift operator ever since. While he waited for his girlfriend in the mall one day in 1995, something came over him as he browsed a few stores. He decided to have one last thrill and steal a pair of socks worth $2.50.[14] He was "enthusiastically apprehended" by a couple of security guards, and because it was his third offense, he was sentenced to life in prison. To pay for the socks he stole, he was fined $2,500. He works at the prison cafeteria getting paid so little he won't have it paid off until he is in his nineties.[15] 45% of people serving a life sentence under three strikes are black. Many are mentally ill and disabled. Three strikes also added $19 billion to California's prison budget.[16] As Rolling Stones stated, the law is cruel and very, very unusual. In fact, it makes no sense at all.

I had the same idea as this man once. When I was younger, I stole a lot, but I had grown up. I had a 4.0, was the president of my college's honor society, and just gave birth to my son. I was working a couple of jobs as I tried to keep my new family afloat and had a couple of volunteer positions, building up my resume, so I could get into a good school after community college. I gave speeches in front of hundreds of people and had received $10,000 in scholarships that year. But I was in the grocery store one day. I got myself a donut from the bakery and thought, no one would suspect anything if I walked out right now. I'm a good girl, a contributing member of society. No one will stop me. For old times sake, I stole the donut. It was thrilling. I haven't stolen since, but because I am white and female, no one thought a thing.

My boss for years working at a Native American fish market explained to me that white privilege means that I can walk into a department store and use the bathroom and browse around without anyone paying any attention to me. If a Native girl did that, eyes would be on her. People would maybe look down on her for using the bathroom and not buying anything or suspect her of stealing. The man who is serving a life sentence for stealing a pair of socks from the mall is black. If he was white, I guarantee he wouldn't be in prison today.

It has been especially appalling throughout my journey with prisoners to learn of the laws that put them away. Unlike crime shows and mystery novels, most people accused of committing a crime never get to meet with a lawyer.[17]

Interrogations are so intense, people give in and plead guilty out of fear. The interrogators are so convinced of the person's guilt, people plead guilty to avoid harsh mandatory sentencing, and plea bargains lock many innocent people away.

When I think of intense, screaming, tortuous interrogations, it is hard to believe that this is happening in my neighborhood. But it is. It is happening here and throughout the United States. Interrogations will go on for days. No police officer wants to put the wrong man behind bars, but when an officer wants justice or is convinced of someone's guilt, they are willing to go to extreme measures to get a confession out of them. One young man, 19 years old and struggling so badly with his mental health that he attempted suicide multiple times, was brought in under false pretenses and questioned for four days. He was accused and screamed at the entire four days and was brought to the crime scene where the violent rape and murder occurred. After the 12th hour on the fourth day, he gave in, sobbing and nodding his head in defeat. He pleaded guilty to a crime he did not commit and would serve the next 19 years for. He was exonerated but lost much of his life.[18] A prison sentence, whether you committed the crime or not, is detrimental to one's life and future opportunities.

False convictions happen frequently. Over 4% of the people on death row, a horrible, monstrous place, are innocent, falsely convicted. That is one in 25.[19] Anthony Ray Hinton was one of these men. In his book, *The Sun Does Shine*, Hinton talks about how he could have gotten out of his over 30-year sentence on death row as an innocent man if he had had the money to pay for a proper attorney during the racist murder trial where he was wrongly convicted.[20] It is often poor people and minorities who end up unfairly going to prison because they were targeted or because they were falsely accused and didn't have enough money to prove their innocence.

The previously mentioned case, a 19-year-old boy who was coerced into pleading guilty, was a special case because of his exoneration. Most falsely convicted prisoners are never able to scrounge up the resources to even have a chance at such a feat. 80% of criminal defendants are too poor to hire a lawyer.[21] Some states won't provide court-appointed lawyers if you make over a certain amount of money each year, and I'm not talking about earning a living wage. In Wisconsin, if you earned more than $3,000 that year, they expect you to afford your own lawyer. Because of this ridiculous law, 11,000 people every year go to court without legal representation.[22] Even if someone does have the resources, such in the case of Anthony Ray Hinton who received help from the Equal Justice Initiative, a group of people fighting to get the falsely convicted off death row among many other pursuits, it is extremely difficult to be re-tried and put in a position for your case to be reconsidered. Even just one person being falsely convicted would be too many people, but this is happening all the time. It is crucial we make changes to criminal justice as this process is not just. Keeping our world safe is too important to continue overlooking this massive violation of equity.

The current system for public defenders doesn't help as they are loaded up with an unmanageable number of cases and paid very little for their work. In our country, being a lawyer is such an esteemed profession that I think we sometimes overlook the possibility of poor working conditions. When we receive help from a court-appointed lawyer, we need them to do everything in their power to help us, but how can these lawyers serve to the best of their ability when they are sometimes working with over 100 clients at a time?[23]

The punishment should fit the crime. People are spending obscene and unjust amounts of time in prison. For someone to get sentenced to life in prison over a pair of socks is obviously wrong, and it is not just this one case. Our current system is missing the point. We want to keep our society safe. With how we incarcerate people now, especially after the war on drugs, we are doing the opposite. Minorities live in fear that they could fall victim to a racist system. When a teenager makes a mistake, they could spend a large portion of their life behind bars and have every opportunity to succeed later in life stripped from them. Going to prison isn't like getting an attitude adjustment and coming out ready to be a productive member of society. Without rehabilitation or a chance for opportunity after prison, any amount of time in prison can seem like a life sentence. We are not keeping our nation safe. With our current criminal justice system, we are actually attacking vulnerable members of society.

UNDER PRESSURE

Bailey,

Got your letter last night and was pleased to receive it. Thank you for writing me! I am 21 years old. I am incarcerated for carjacking, grand theft, assault with deadly weapon, and felony evading. However, that sounds a lot worse than what really happened. No one was hurt whatsoever, but due to technicalities of the law, I was sadly charged with certain crimes. I worked after school and on the weekends sometimes at my friend's dairy as an attempt by him and his family to keep me out of trouble, and I grew to love all the different aspects of that job. I was arrested at that dairy and spent my first night ever in juvenile hall while working there. I very much wish I was still able to join the military upon my release, but unfortunately due to my felony prosecutions, I don't believe that's a reality anymore.

I wish I had learned about substance abuse and what life could be like if you chose to make the wrong decisions and end up in jail or prison, leaving you with limited job opportunities when released back to society. As a kid, you're always under pressure to be cool/popular, so you do these things that give off the impression of being cool even if you know that's not really you. And then slowly, you change, and that "cool" life actually becomes who you are and the way you act/behave without you even realizing it or admitting it because to you, it's not a big deal or problem. Sadly kids like I was will continue to fall for the interpreted cool reality of your life style and either end up in prison or jail for stretches at a time or end up in dead-end jobs working 6 days a week to barely make it in your bills, scraping by due to lack of interest of education while in high school or college cause you were too busy partying or getting high. All of this is an attempt to mask your pain or create a false identity of yourself to stay in a bracket of a "cool" social ladder.

I have a lot more to share in the future if you're interested. Have a good day Bailey.
Kelly Evans

NO EVIDENCE AT ALL

Hey Bailey

That's crazy that your brother goes to the same high school as me. What are the odds of that happening? My appeal is going good. They are reviewing my case now and from the sound of it, I might be home soon I hope. The situation was that my older brother and I never got along in life, so one day I was with my mother at Walmart doing some shopping, and the next thing I know he said I touched his daughter in a bad manner, and he was going to turn me in to the cops. So he did that, and I'm here now. They convicted me with hearsay and no evidence at all. I took a polygraph test, and it said everything was negative for everything I did. But I can not use that in court. You are the first person I have told besides my family that I did not commit this case. She could not even identify me in trial. In long words, I got fucked at the end. Sorry for swearing.

I'm 23 and have no kids at all. I got raised in a good family. When I got out of school, I worked in a factory welding parts together. I had a girlfriend when I got locked up, but after 2 years in prison she left me and let me go. We still talk sometimes, but it's hard for me to let go. I don't even know why I'm telling you this, maybe to get it off my mind. I did not think you would write me back. Thanks for the letter and hope to hear from you soon.

Tobias Markoff

THE TRUE MEANING BEHIND THE EVENTS

Bailey Bailey Bailey,

I'm so happy to have got your letter today, and I'm so beyond grateful for the paperwork you sent by Tony Robbins. The paperwork and the Rising Strong book means the world to me cause, Bailey, I been away 4 ½ years and no one has invested in my growth or supported the person I'm becoming. Not that anyone owes me their support and not that anyone is entitled to invest in me, but I had many so-called friends 4½ years ago, and I knew many people, but now, all I have is my higher power, my mom, myself, and a new friend name Bailey. Funny thing is I never even met you yet so for you to believe in my growth and invest in my growth, for you to support the person I am and support the person I'm becoming, it all means the world to me.

Bailey, the way I chose to view my incarceration since the beginning has been a blessing from god. I prayed for proper perspective. I prayed for deep understanding. Being away brought those things into my life. The story I told myself freed me. It empowered me. My truth has literally set me free, and I must continue to live in that reality.

The two guys I held up they was not in any way a part of the lifestyle I chose, so instead of revenge, they called the police. I could of easily been or even be that guy like many disturbed men in this place holding everyone but myself accountable, saying man I got snitched on, or I'm here cause of someone snitching, but divine intervention guided me into understanding the true meaning behind the events, which were accountability and responsibility. In the beginning, I had an epiphany. It was my actions that led up to my conviction, not two statements. All I hoped for was getting a fair sentence, a sentence that matched the severity of my crime. I was caught red-handed, so I was prepared for my consequences. My mother hired a paid lawyer. I told him I do not want to fight this. Just get me a fair sentence. He didn't agree with my attitude.

I was prepared to do about 8 years straight, and of course, many states and many cities and counties are very different in their court system. Bailey, I was facing 21 to 45 years in prison at 85%, just turned 19 years old a month before. The courts first offer for me was 30 years at 85%. My lawyer got me 23 years at 50%. That's 11 ½ years for armed robbery, and I hurt no one in my city. That sentence is more severe than the actual crime. They did not consider anything else.

Bailey, hear me out. I legit have an uncle Andre who drove up to a gas station on a bike and shot a man several times on camera. He had a public defender, and he only did 6 years for attempted murder. Now do you understand how I could take that reality and trap myself in a negative space. There are many men here now doing less time than myself for the same crime and some with less time and more severe cases, but I humbled myself telling myself had I not run around engaging in that type of activity then I wouldn't see the others who may have less time for the same crime as myself. Had I not did what I done and lived how I lived, the courts wouldn't have had the very opportunity to oversentence me so unfairly. It was more important for me to hold myself accountable for my role then to blame cause even if blame is blameworthy, blame doesn't empower or free us. It's like I knew this before I actually understood it, and one thing I believe is we as people will forgive ourselves long before we will forgive others. Its so easy to blame everyone and everything.

There was a guy in my county jail who got 7 years for armed robbery, and he attacked his victims. I could have been bitter, but I was more hurt in all honesty cause although I done something wrong and against the law and stupid, I was hurt almost feeling defeated in terms of getting a fair sentence. The states first offer to me of 30 years at 85%, that's 20 plus years for an armed robbery and no one got hurt. How in the world is that a fair sentence when my uncle shot a man on camera and only did 6 years for attempted murder? I'm not trying to downplay armed robbery. To hold someone at gunpoint is a scary and terrible thing to do. It's been done to me. I been robbed and, Bailey, I'm sharing this all to say I could be or could have been bitter about my incarceration, but I'm not, and I feel Tony Robbins on his teaching of the meanings we give the events in our life. I feel Tony deeply. I agree with his knowledge, and it lives in my muscles anytime I'm sharing my story. I feel freed and empowered, and at the same time, I'm possibly empowering whoever listens.

Dr. Phil who I admire and look up to says, "We cannot change something we won't acknowledge." So with that being said, look at me now. I grown apart from that lifestyle I once lived, and I grown apart from fair weather friends. I'm able to change course. I have acknowledged the danger and dysfunction in that lifestyle I come from. I have acknowledged the fact that my so-called friends aren't true friends to me. I think so highly of you. I don't know women like you. You're becoming a best friend to me.

Peace and love.
Sincerely,
Quintavius

WHERE I STRUGGLED

Bailey,

It's nice to get some mail from somebody. I am 22 years old with two children I had senior year. Shortly after, I dropped out. I loved high school, but where I struggled wasn't with the teachers or curriculum. It was with my past and my emotions. The schools would tell you they cared about your future, but they didn't have any programs or classes or people who could help you overcome your past so you could move on. I am currently in GED classes and will obtain it within a few months. I am going to get my Associates in Liberal Arts, and I will work towards my goal of being a rehab counselor for teens and young adults. I am currently incarcerated for agg. discharge of a firearm and agg. battery. Someone kicked in my door while my son was home so I retaliated. Happy Mothers Day if you are a mother. Blessings.

Ian Wagner

IF I KNEW MY RIGHTS

Hello Mrs. McManus,

As you know my name is Dale. I am 21 years of age, but what you don't know is that I was arrested at 18, 2 days after graduation. I enjoyed everything about high school except homework, but what I most enjoyed was my music and dance classes. I worked at a dance studio teaching hip-hop part time and worked at a truck wash full time. I would have started audio engineering classes. That didn't happen because I was arrested, which leads me to what I wish I learned. I wish I paid attention in my government class and knew my rights instead of going by what I seen on TV. If I knew to keep my mouth shut, I wouldn't be here.

I'm incarcerated because I thought if I told a lie that was different from what I was being accused of they would let me go. Now I am in prison because of my own lie. I shot myself in the foot with my ignorance where if I had said nothing, I would have went free because what I was being accused of was a lie too, and they had no evidence to connect. I had sex with a man's wife. He found out and as revenge, accused me of raping his stepdaughter, which wasn't true, so I accusd her of touching and pursuing me, but being 18, it didn't matter. I was convicted of child molestation (she was 14).

The prosecutor said he would have had to drop the case if I said nothing. I am now fighting my appeals, hoping and praying to go home.

Dale Walker

MUSIC WAS ON

Bailey,

I really do appreciate you taking the time to write me. So I have a long story for only being 20 years old. I dropped out of school my 7th grade year and started using meth. It was only a matter of a time before I was spending time in detention and doing time in OYA [Oregon Youth Authority]. I got out of OYA in 2016 and was only out for 9 months when I was driving late one night, raining outside, with a homegirl of mine in the passenger seat. Music was on. It was around 2am, and I went to pass a semi and hit a motorcycle head on. I kinda panicked and did not stop. I drove the car a few miles, pulled over and called a friend for a ride. Within 24 hours, my name and picture was on Fox 12 news most wanted. The guy on the motorcycle had died. I got caught 2 days later and was charged with manslaughter. I got sentenced to 12 years. I have an amazing 10 month old daughter. I am a 20 year old young man who had a car accident and has made some mistakes. I am really going to use these next 12 years to better myself. I'm not a bad person. This is not the life I wanted. Some days are harder than others, but all I can do is stay positive. Thank you. Can't wait to hear back from you.

Sincerely,
Harrison Paul Jones

BURIED ALIVE

Okay, so let me give you a hug.

It's Friday. I sent you a quick email last night. You asked how the lawsuit was going . . . I am still waiting for the judge to grant me judgment to proceed against the main defendant at trial. I have been waiting for some time now, but also understand that a lot has slowed down due to the virus. The courts even put cases on hold cause of this reason. I just pray that I can go to trial on it soon and win a judgment so that I can finally get the appropriate legal counsel to get me home. That is the ultimate objective. As for, is there anything you can help with umm let me see . . . do you have a magic wand? How about a key? Do you have a key to let me go home? Yeah, I know. If it were only that easy, huh?

It sucks, my friend, that individuals such as myself have been in prison so fucken long, and because one does not have the financial means to get the right attorney to get home, we get buried and lost in the system, UNJUSTLY. I know I made a lot of mistakes when I was young, but definitely that is not a reason to bury a young man alive. I am not in prison for taking someone's life or physically harming anyone. Rather I was young, addicted to drugs and looking for quick money to party. I am in prison for masked armed robbery and discharging a gun around people (I shot in the air). Yet, I was treated like a terrorist cause I was young, Hispanic, and grew up in a rough neighborhood involved in gangs.

Bailey, I see guys come into prison everyday for murder and get way less time than me. It's one of those WTF (what the fuck) moments. It makes no sense. Yet I am living proof of it. So yeah, I am always sad and bitter at the thought of my reality. But it is what it is. I just have to keep my head up and stay focused, never giving up on love, faith, or life. And at the end of the day, in a strange way I am grateful for being removed from society for some time cause it has allowed me to see the beauty in special moments, in something as simple as your son sleeping over with your mom for a few nights and having that special time with her. That to me, my friend, is something special and beautiful in its rawest form. And now you just made me a little teary eyed! Oh well. Even that I embrace and appreciate. Let me wrap this up here so I can get this out. I will chat with you a bit tomorrow. Take care, and hope you sleep well. Strong hug, love always.

Your friend,
Dominic

NEVER BEEN IN TROUBLE

Dear Bailey,

It was great to hear from you! I am glad that you enjoyed the card I sent. I enjoy the depth of your letters! They never fail to put a smile on my face or at least make me ponder.

Bailey, I was also grateful that you shared your feelings about a racial issue . . . Racism is real but everyone does not share the same viewpoint. Does not mean that they are a racist. Certain facts do stand out. Certain facts do stand out. In America, whites outnumber blacks. Whites actually commit more crime than blacks. That's just the law of average. If that is a fact then why is between 65 and 70 percent of the prison system black? That in itself is creating a problem because a lot of the brightest minds are in prison. If those bright minds were set on the right path and used to achieve and accomplish things in the proper order of things, then the world would benefit. Instead, they are . . .

Crime is real and thus the need for a criminal justice system is well founded. As a well-read person whom has taken college courses, I'm sure that you have been exposed to or soon will be exposed to Soc. classes in which they talk about the Stanford clinical trial where half the students were used as inmates and the other half used as prison guards. The guards treated their own classmates different just based on the fact that they were given total control over someone else's life. People understand the need for the criminal justice system and agree that those incarcerated should be treated humanly, but they often refuse to acknowledge the corruption that seems to overcome humans when they are placed in certain positions of authority. Studies have been done that show people age out of crime. If that is true, why do we have people in prison that have reached a certain age? Not only that, anyone whom has been in prison more than 20 years is not the same as the person that the system sent to prison. Why is that person still in prison?

Then you must ask what does the criminal justice system expect to happen to someone that was incarcerated in the 90s and is not released until well into the 2020s. No access to advancements in society, no work place skills, no means to offset the stigma of prison. Alas, the system set that person up for failure. It just so happens that most of the people facing these problems are black.

Bailey, on the prison unit that I am on, there are between 50 and 100 people who came to prison when they were 17 and younger and have been incarcerated for over 25 years. In Texas, there are over 100 prison units. (That's the average per unit. 50-100.) So that's between 5,000 and 10,000 people that face such a problem. The majority of them are black. Should most of them have been sent to prison? Yes! Bailey, I freely acknowledge that for my part in the crime that I was involved in, I should have went to prison. Should I have been incarcerated for 25 years? No!

What's funny is that in 1996 there was a white dude that was a year older than me that also had been charged by the law "guilty by association of murder." He was sentenced to 15 years in prison. I had never been in trouble, but I was sentenced to 50 to life. Prison is a big business. The unjustness of the system. Its unfairness should be exposed.

Until I hear from you, keep manifesting the peace that you want. Depth and creativity is a part of you.

With best wishes and love,
DeWayne

MY FREEDOM

Bailey McMantis,

How have you been, Bailey? I want you to know that my slack in writing has been inexcusable. I've been working and not idle. I've been through an emotional wringer, a spiritual doldrum, doubting so much about things I truly have no control of.

Let me tell you about it. This will be a catharsis.

I graduated from the Horizon Program in December of last year. We were moved out and others were moved in January of this year.

I left on a high note.

But it did not last.

I had two suggestions (or ideas, thoughts or whatever you want to call them) that entered my mind that were a direct challenge to my desire for my future.

One concerned my freedom.

I was presented with the idea that I may very well NOT get out of prison. I really don't want to go into detail, but lets just say it was profound.

Shortly afterwards I was, in the same way, presented with the idea that I would NOT be married.

The combination of these two ideas overwhelmed me and threatened to turn my world upside down.

I was then asked to RETURN to the Horizon Program. I knew that it was an honor to return, no to be asked to return.

And I accepted of course.

But this was at one of my lowest points of my incarcerated life. I saw myself doing what I'd always done when I was depressed.

I turned inward.

I withdrew from the world. Into myself.

But God is the best of planners.

I was being recalled to Horizon because one of the new members had experienced a rough patch. But the crazy thing was that that young man had credited me with planting the seed that eventually lead him to Horizon in the first place.

But something happened. For the first time in the history of the Horizon Program, a man was dismissed from the program AND returned to the program in the same class (year).

But God is the best of planners.

By returning this young man to the gram I was presented from that withdrawal from the world that was expected of me.

As well as that young man having guidance and counsel from someone he knew and respected.

I'm sure I told you that the type of sentence I have would have to do ½ of my sentence before I would be eligible for parole consideration.

I had a 40 year sentence I received in 2002. So, June 2022 I would be eligible for parole for the first time.

The process typically begins 90 days before you "date." The parole headquarters would notify the unit parole representative and I would be interviewed to collect addresses, phone numbers, plans, job prospects, etc.

THEN, this info, once collected would be turned over to the regional office and I, because I had served twenty or more years, would be interviewed by a parole commissioner, who would be the lead voter on a three person panel that would decide if and when I would be released.

The problem was (and you know I would find one) that I was three weeks away from my date and no one had seen me.

Talk about panic! Remember the "idea" I had wrote about not getting out of prison?

So I wrote to the unit parole rep. On my unit, and she informed me that I WAS NOT under review nor was I eligible for review. Now, remember the review process should have began 90 days before the date. Her response came to me roughly 7 days before the date the review should have been complete.

It wasn't until 26 days AFTER that I was seen for the preliminary interview.

And seven weeks after the date passed that I finally sat down for a video conference with a lady who identified herself as the lead voter on a 3 person panel that would decide whether or not to release me.

She asked five very good questions and gave me ample opportunity to answer. She asked if I had any questions (I did not).

She wrapped the interview up by notifying me that I would receive an answer by 30 days.

My answer came less than 20 HOURS LATER!

I was granted parole, Bailey.

I'll close this letter saying thanks for being there for me. Thanks for all you've done.

Much love,
Flloyd Ike Williams

FACTS ABOUT SENTENCING

1 in 25 people on death row are falsely convicted.[24]

Mass incarceration cost taxpayers nearly "$87 billion in 2015 for roughly the same level of public safety achieved in 1978 for $5.5 billion."[25]

Stanford Law School wrote about their the three strikes law, "Project clients have been given life sentences for offenses including stealing one dollar in loose change from a parked car, possessing less than a gram of narcotics, and attempting to break into a soup kitchen." 45% of people serving a life sentence under three strikes are black. Many are mentally ill and disabled. Three strikes also added $19 billion to California's prison budget.[26]

Most people accused of a crime never get to meet with a lawyer.[27]

Blacks are six times more likely to go to prison than whites.[28]

PRISON LIFE

When a person is sent to prison, this method of intervention is sending them straight into a traumatic environment. To take a person out of society and send them into a violent and dangerous place should take great speculation and certainty that there is absolutely nowhere else for them to go. Alcatraz was a place where only the worst of the worst criminals went. The most dangerous people who should not be allowed to co-exist with everyone else, who create unsafe communities. Now, we have regular people, young people, who make mistakes being sent to prison, thrown into communities and even cells with murderers, rapists, and violent criminals.

Bryan Stevenson, one of my personal heroes, founded the Equal Justice Initiative. He and his team fight for criminal justice reform, racial justice, and public education reform. In his book *Just Mercy*, Stevenson shared a story I will never forget. Charlie, a fourteen-year-old boy, found himself in an Alabama jail cell. His grandmother contacted Stevenson and begged him to help this wonderful boy who never got in trouble but was now facing murder charges.[1]

Charlie's mother had been dating a man who lived with them for the previous year and a half. His mother, like most women in abusive relationships, made excuses for her boyfriend, saying the reason he was angry and drank so much was because his wife and children had been killed in a car accident. Charlie watched his mother fade away, smiling less and losing the happy, vibrant parts of herself. Her boyfriend had never hurt Charlie, but he was unkind to him and violent with his mother.[2]

One night, Charlie and his mom sat at the kitchen table playing cards when her boyfriend came home drunk. Charlie's mother didn't say anything, but Charlie could tell she was mad. Her boyfriend noticed the anger too. He walked up to her and punched her in the face. As she fell to the floor, her head hit the metal kitchen counter. The boyfriend went upstairs and fell asleep.[3]

Blood poured onto the floor. For a few minutes, Charlie tried to stop the bleeding with paper towels. Because she was unconscious and bleeding so badly, soaking the paper towels and Charlie's clothes, he thought she was dying. He had only called the police once before after an event like this, but his mother had been conscious and guided him through it. The only phone in the house was located in his mother's bedroom where her boyfriend slept.[4]

Charlie was weeping, and his nose had started to bleed as it had when he experienced fear as a child. He knew he had to do something. He went upstairs to call 911, but as he reached for the phone, he saw the man who had been so horrible to his mother—the one who had probably just killed her. He reached underneath the phone into the drawer below, and he found the gun he knew the boyfriend kept there. He pointed it at the man and shot him. The gun was so loud, it terrified him, and he almost toppled over. He called the police and waited with his mom downstairs.[5]

The abusive man living in Charlie's home was a police officer. Not only did the judge try Charlie as an adult, he gave Charlie the death sentence.[6]

When Stevenson traveled to speak with Charlie, he was being held at a county jail. Stevenson thought him to be too short, thin, and frightened to be even fourteen years old. When Charlie was called in for the legal visit, he was completely unresponsive. He moved his head, but showed no emotion. Stevenson became concerned for this child. He tried tactics he had used before like offering to buy some food or asking about things Charlie liked. After a while, Stevenson took a chance and put his arm around the boy. Charlie gave in and started sobbing, his sobs becoming more uncontrollable the longer he spoke. He confessed that he had been gang raped every night he had been in the county jail.[7]

Stevenson agreed to work on Charlie's case. He helped to make sure Charlie was never hurt in jail again. He defended Charlie, and the case was dropped to a juvenile case. Charlie was still sent to an adult prison but was released in just a few years.[8] Stevenson has done incredible work to protect children who are incarcerated and even change the policies that send them to prison in the first place. There is much more to this story. I highly suggest reading *Just Mercy* so you can read it for yourself. Charlie is not the only person to face horrific mistreatment upon incarceration, but he was one of the few to have help from Bryan Stevenson. Most people end up with no support and have to face the mistreatment alone.

We cannot ignore crime, but we also cannot continue to incarcerate people the way we are now. In two hundred years, I believe American society will look back on this time and think it is quite strange how we treated our criminals. It is not only issues with sentencing or stigmatization upon release. Like Charlie, many people who commit crimes experience horrific conditions during their time in jail or prison. Just last year, one civil rights lawyer in Florida received 30 to 60 letters a week from prisoners who witnessed and experienced beatings, stabbings, and lack of medical services, and in a single week, five people were murdered in Mississippi state prisons.[9]

Based on research studies in 2002 and 2004, 56 percent of state prisoners, 45 percent of federal prisoners, and 64 percent of jail inmates had mental health problems, and a huge portion of those people reported symptoms of a mental disorder such as a personality or developmental disorder. 49 percent of state prisoners, 40 percent of federal prisoners, and 60 percent of jail inmates exhibited these symptoms.[10] A sheriff in Nashville said, "We are arresting people who have no idea what the laws are or the rules are because they're off their medications. You'd never arrest someone for a heart attack, but you're comfortable arresting someone who is diagnosed mentally ill. No other country in the world is doing it this way."[11] This is recognizably wrong. Prisons are not equipped to handle the influx of mentally ill. Staff members and prisoners are both suffering.

In 2019, suicide accounted for 8 percent of deaths in state and federal prisons and 30 percent of death in local jails.[12] One study found that 41 percent of these suicides happened in people who were currently or had recently been in solitary confinement, which exacerbates symptoms of mental illness.[13] In many cases, family and friends will try to warn the facility about their loved one's mental illness even going so far as to bring their mediations to the jail. A 2019 article in Prison Legal News said, "It's not uncommon for such prisoners to wind up in isolation, naked and smearing feces around their cell."[14] This is exactly what I've heard from my pen pals about living with the mentally ill in prison. Prisons aren't equipped to handle the sheer volume of mental illness cases coming to them.

And if something bad happens to you in prison, getting legal help is nearly impossible. Rights for people in prison exist. Exercising these rights is a different story.

My dear friend, known in this book as Dominic, was sexually abused by a prison employee. To fight the abuse that occurred, he had to go through the court. By doing this, he had to come out with the fact that his safety rights had been compromised. He faced scrutiny from the prison for doing so. He also faced scrutiny from his peers. Fellow inmates didn't understand why he had a problem with the abuse. They thought Dominic was lucky for getting female attention. Any victim of abuse will immediately understand how hard this would be.

If facing his peers and prison employees was not enough, his fear of making the information known was held against him in court. It was said that he should have requested help immediately. I don't know one person who has experienced sexual abuse who had the courage to ask for help right away. Not one.

My friend worked on the case on his own without resources for a long time before it was set into motion. If he found a book in the prison library that seemed helpful, it would disappear the next day. The prison was working against him. He didn't have access to the internet like a person outside of prison would, and it was very unclear what his rights were and what he needed to do to move forward with fighting the injustice he experienced.

Society tends to think people in prison have all this free time, but there is more to prison than just sitting in a cell. You are counted multiple times every day, and when the signal sounds, everyone stops what they're doing to line up. It can also be so loud during the day that it is hard to focus, so people will stay up late at night when they have tasks like studying to complete.[15] People are required by the Federal Bureau of Prisons to work during their sentence. They work as plumbers, groundskeepers, food service staff, and have various other jobs throughout the prison.[16] For my friend to find the time to put together this case entirely on his own took tremendous courage and skill. His time management skills, desire to learn, and willingness to face his own demons far surpasses that which I've seen in most people outside of prison.

To be a victim of sexual abuse in an environment where everyone around you is against you, believes you are in the wrong, and is actively working to fight against your case—this is what it's like for people who try to exercise their rights in prison.

Living conditions in prison vary depending on your location. I hear stories of living conditions that are okay, where people come into a space that is basically clean and they are allowed access to things like time outside. I also hear stories about people showing up to a new cell covered in food and urine and mouse poop with the window broken and no heat in the middle of winter.

In the late 1800s, African Americans replaced immigrants and took up almost the entire prison population in America. These inmates were abused and brutally overworked. With no access to medical care and exposure to disease, death rates were high.[17] Almost 100 years later in the 1970s, the Attica Prison Riot in New York exposed injustices such as prison abuse and policies that made prison life miserable including only allowing inmates one shower per week and one roll of toilet paper per month. In the 1990s, prison abuse was again exposed at the Pelican Bay State Prison where a lawsuit, Madrid v. Gomez, exposed rights violations and abuse.[18] These cries for humane treatment from prisoners in the United States have been met with minor changes, but the cycle of prison abuse continues today.

Most inmates are not dangerous or psychotic in the stereotypical way people tend to stigmatize prisoners. There are a lot of very normal people making mistakes in the world and being sent to prison. The experience of trauma in prison is more than just harmful. It is wrong. By allowing these people, who will be returning back to our communities and are citizens of the United States, to be in a situation where they go through trauma and decrease their mental health and ability to function in the world, we are decreasing the functionality of our society. People come out traumatized and often commit other crimes and return to prison, leaving their families suffering and their children more likely to go to prison themselves.

Some argue against rehabilitation and better living conditions because they don't want to waste money on people who commit crimes, but if we looked at the situation with enough distance to see the data, we would realize that simply sending people to prison costs taxpayers more money than rehabilitating would. We would actually save money by rehabilitating, providing education, and creating non-traumatic living conditions because recidivism rates decrease dramatically when we do so. Outside of the monetary cost, the cost of losing a person to a string of prison sentences is devastating to families, communities, and incarcerated individuals. The fact is, people who go to prison almost always rejoin society. What do we want that coexistence to look like? It is time to start treating them with the decency every human deserves.

Prison is not supposed to be fun. With the current attitude toward people who are in incarcerated in America, I'm not sure we are evolved enough as a society to create an environment where people can truly come back to their authentic selves. But I have a problem with violating each other. I have a problem with doing things that make absolutely no sense. Nothing about how we treat prisoners in our country is logical. My hope is that we do not need to wait two hundred years to see it. That we can open our eyes to it right now and make a change. We ought to at least try.

A GENEROUS EYE

Dear Bailey,

Today an officer caught a guy crawling into an air duct in the ceiling in the building next to ours. Sometimes I'm amazed by the ignorance of some of these guys in here. I guess it's their thought process that baffles me the most. I guess all I can do is ask God to help them. Out of nowhere yesterday, my celly came to me with a Bible and showed me a scripture, Proverbs 22:9. "He who has a generous eye will be blessed for he gives of his bread to the poor." He said this is you. I asked why he said that, and he said he sits back and watches me always looking out for these young kids. I'm always helping the less fortunate guys in here. My celly is an old chicano dude. It was very nice of him to tell me that.

It would be nice to get blessed. I guess there are some ways I've been blessed. My babies are safe, I met you, I'm alive. You never know, you may be an angel sent to help me be a better person, to help me make better decisions. Or maybe God brought me into your life to help you. I say that because I did write you first. Lol. What kind of bad or negative things are going on in your life that you wish you could make better? What are some things you don't like about yourself? Is there anything you like or dislike about me? There are a lot of things I don't like about myself. One thing is not being the daddy that my babies deserve. I let people take advantage of my kindness. I always pick the wrong people to be friends with and especially the wrong girls to be in a relationship with. I trust people too easily. I have a really bad habit of helping other people, knowing it's gonna bite me in the butt later on. Do you have any of these problems? There are so many good things about me too.

I can't sleep good in here at night, so I just stay up super late and write you letters. Mostly because I know how much you enjoy reading. I hope you don't mind all the letters. I really want to get to know you. You seem like a wonderful person. The food here sucks. I try not to eat it as much as possible. I wouldn't even want my dog to eat this stuff. Funny story, so the dudes in here always ask why Im always up until 4:00am writing. I tell them I'm writing my pen pal. They say I'm full of it. So I finally broke down and showed them your pic. They gave me a hard time because they don't believe such a pretty girl would write a convict. I told them it took me a long long time and patience to finally meet a special person like you. Most of the guys in here are just pigs. They always have nasty things to say about a female. You really have to be careful who you talk to in here. Anyways they are a bit jealous. Then, they ask me stupid questions. But you did get a few compliments. One thing about these guys in here is they are very dependent because they have never lived a life with responsibility. So I chose to take it upon myself to school these guys on how to make better people of themselves. I tell them they have to help themselves and need to take on some sort of responsibility. I've had dozens of people tell me I don't deserve to be in here. What if God has me in here for a reason? Maybe I'm in here to help other people change their lives, or at least teach them what I can. Give them the right advice. Make them better people.
   Till next time.

Yours Truly,
Jason Moore

BIANNUAL SHAKEDOWN

Bailey

I just had to write you to say a very hearty 'Thank you' for the three books that you sent. I've already read 15 Invaluable Laws of Growth over the past four days. That book truly opened my mind to a codified set of rules that govern leadership and growth. Bailey, I really needed that book because I am in the position to be a mentor and leader in here. I am and should be judged on my personal qualities and effectiveness. And as I let others read this book, they have a more objective 'ruler' with which to judge and measure me. And I'll have the wherewithal to judge those I seek to mentor me. This comes at a very important point of my development. I come up for my first parole hearing in 2 ½ to 3 years so it is time for me to really start put into place and practice the habits and attitudes and discipline that will carry me forward. Bailey, I do not believe it was accidental that you were brought into my life.

Everyone is preparing for the biannual lockdown/shakedown again. Preparation includes getting rid of excess weight (books!) because we will be required to carry our property roughly 100 yards to the gym and back. And guys want the load to be as light as possible. I, myself, have a "lighting restriction" that qualifies me to place my property on a cart with others who have such restrictions. This creates a business opportunity in that I can charge others without a restriction to have their bags put on the cart as if they were my bags, and it saves the owner from carrying them. I usually charge $1.00 per bag, and that's 3 ramen soups! These come in handy after the first 6 or 7 days of peanut butter and bologna!

Thank you Bailey, and I pray you and yours are blessed as you have blessed others.

Your appreciative friend,
Floyd

QUESTIONS WHY

Freedom taken
Life forsaken.
Steel bars
Painful scars,
Mental strains
Waist chains.
Concrete walls
Collect calls,
Nothing fair,
Hard to bear
Mind games
Nicknames
Count bells
Stair wells
Masked strangers
Constant dangers
Jingling keys
Trembling knees
Lonely hours
Faith sours
Years wasted
Hope tasted
Questions why
Then I cry

By Dominic Sanchez

ONE PERSON

Bailey

It really does my heart good to know that you enjoyed the card I sent to you. I hope that you made some beautiful memories for yourself and your family.

I have been thinking about a phrase that I had been using a lot back in 2016-2017 with someone that was preparing to leave this unit and transfer to another. At some point it became clear to me that he was absorbing everything I was showing him and was trying to relate to others but was finding that second part frustrating. I told him to find one person who understood and teach them. That person would then go on to teach others. He may have to wade through 10's of people who just don't get it, but if you find ONE that does "get it," there will be exponential growth of your message if you focus on that teacher.

Bailey I truly hope you and your loved ones are good. I'm gearing up for my first parole hearing two years from now. I will have done a mandatory 20 years on a 40 year sentence. Because I'll have done 20 years I will get to see "The Commissioner" whose vote carries a lot of weight. So there's that to consider.

Please keep me in your prayers as you all will be in mine.

Your friend,
Floyd Ike Williams

SUICIDE SQUAD

Bailey,

So you are a nanny now? What in the heeelll lol. Bailey, you do everything lol. Have you ever heard of a cartoon show called American Dad? You would be the alien because in every show, no matter where they go, the alien works everywhere lol. I wouldn't be surprised if one day I wake up to a flash from a flash light and I hear, "Hey! Name and number!" I look and I'm like, "What in the hell? Bailey?" Lmao.

Now that I think about it, just so you know, everybody can get hired here just look at the website. All units need from guards to counselors. In the type of unit I stay in you work 4 days and rest 4. If you ever work a job in Texas prison, you will get it. You should come, bring me a cell phone and from there I'll just send you money lol. You know I paid 1600 for my first one? If you ever visit my world, you will see how fucked up it is. You will have to get used to getting jacked off on lol.

You would also see that Texas prison is out of there. Mice everywhere, roaches. Water and power always going off. Have you ever seen Suicide Squad? You remember Will Smith when he wasn't trying to come out the cell or some shit so about 5 guards fully suited with a shield ran in his cell and beat his ass? Well that's what really happens lol. Except we get sprayed with like 3 cans of spray first and then they run in and beat us like an alcoholic husband lol.

As for what else I got going on. Well, I'm just trying to draw and unsuccessfully hustle to eat big so I can work out and get my fine on. I'm just chillin though. Not much I can do. Oh yea. I got on that WriteAPrisoner again. You know what I was thinking earlier? I was thinking it was pretty cool and crazy that the person who has first hit me up on WriteAPrisoner my first time on is still talking to me :). That would be you. How nice lol.

Hope to hear from you soon.

Much love, loyalty, respect.
Matthew Navarro

P.S. Can you help me get this book [Meister Manual for Prisoners' Lawsuits by David J. Meister]? I have been collecting everything I need to file a lawsuit on the state because we are in solitary and there is rules that is priority to fulfill recreation for us. Meaning that, for our mental health we have to come out for an hour which we do not get. My depression gets worse and I will file a lawsuit for all of us to be able to come out. If you can, that would help me a lot! Thank you.

LITERALLY IN TEARS

Hey Bay Bay,

I hope you don't mind the new nickname I gave you. I had you on my mind so I figured I need to write you.

My babies still haven't wrote me. My heart is broken. I feel like maybe I should just give up. My heart doesn't have any quit in it though. I had court last week. The courts gave me back my money I had in my pockets when I got arrested. Almost nine hundred bucks.

Everybody was so sad when I left. They all thought I was leaving for good. A lot of my youngsters were literally in tears when I left. I was gone for three days. When I came back, there was a huge line of inmates waiting for me at the gate. They were so happy I was back. I've never seen nothing like it, how much of a positive impact I really am on these guys. I'm not gonna lie to you and try to act tough. It made me feel a little emotional inside. It made me wonder how these guys would be affected if I wouldn't have come back. Only God knows. It goes to show that God has blessed me with qualities that are life changing for these guys. Maybe not long term changes but maybe changes for the time being, in which I pray could lead to long-term change.

What are your thoughts on this? Why do I feel like I'm working harder at helping other people change than I am helping myself change? Because I am far from a perfect person. Don't you think God would want me to focus more on myself than others? Who knows. I have so many of my own issues, I don't know how to handle myself. Is it because I know how they feel? I don't know. Is it me or is it God that makes me so selfless? I've been told I need to stop helping others. More times than I can count. So do you have a good relationship with your parents. What are they like?

They must be proud of the woman you've become.

Truly yours always & forever,
Jason

SENT TO HELL

Bailey

I wanted to write to you about what I call "The Demon in Hell Mentality." This is about how some prison guards view their jobs and how they carry out their responsibilities.

First, one must understand that we aren't sent to prison to be punished. That would surprise a lot of people, but it's true. Instead, we are sent to prison as punishment. There's a very big difference. But many many people think this is a false dichotomy. A contrivance on the part of inmates and "bleeding hearts." But we're not sent to prison for punishment, not to be punished, but instead we're sent here as punishment for our crimes. The time is our punishment. The time and all that you lose with it.

Statistics tell us that most crime, in fact the overwhelming majority of crime, is committed by males between the ages of 19 and 40 (some say 35). This is when young men are uncertain of themselves and, as a result, overreact and underthink everything. And these are the men who are overrepresented in the prison system.

Back in the day, prison was hyper-violent. The gangs that were formed were for survival. Strength in numbers. So much strength was gained by those swelling numbers, survival turned into oppression. But even that operated as a kind of check on behavior. There were certain things you just wouldn't do. Certain things you wouldn't say. As crazy as it may sound, this worked to enforce peace.

Virtually everything was separated along racial lines. Even the names of the gangs: Mexican mafia, The Black Guerilla Family, The Aryan Brotherhood, etc. Each group had their own territory, their own justice, their own view of world history and even their own vocabulary. And every new arrival was sized up for conscription. And not just conscription, for membership. These organizations needed bodies true enough, canon fodder if you will. But they also needed other things. And each new boot (called 'new boots' because you could tell they had just arrived by the condition of their boots) was weighed to gauge his potential for whatever he could provide. Each group was responsible for the discipline of their kind. Not just their members but their race. Everyone was expected to know their place. And while there were surely outbreaks of violence, extreme violence sometimes, the system worked.

Then two things happened that turned everything on its head. Really, it was three things. One happened on the inside, and two happened on the outside and came inside.

The first thing was a federal lawsuit known as Ruiz v. Estelle. A sweeping, landscape-changing event that literally reshaped and reorganized prisons in Texas and rippled throughout the country. Estelle was the Director of the Texas Department of Corrections (T.D.C.). He oversaw a sprawling prison complex that encompassed about 20 units and hundreds of thousands of acres of farmland across the state of Texas. Tens of thousands of chickens, pigs, cows and horses. All fed, cared for, and slaughtered by inmates.

Then there were the crops. Cotton galore, vegetables of all kinds. All of this went to feed and clothe inmates. So from a business standpoint, T.D.C. was truly a successful operation. The envy of other prisons and states. But on the inside, it was a horror show. The lack of medical doctors, dentists, and access to courts to complain about those lacks was unheard of. Not to mention the brutality of the system. From guards on inmates as well as inmates on inmates. By 1984, a new area in T.D.C. was created called administrative segregation. Before then, there was only solitary. The hole. But it wasn't for long-term lock up.

Ruiz's lawsuit and the consolidation of other lawsuits into Ruiz's suit lead to the creation of "Seg." as it's called now. But it also revolutionized T.D.C. in that oversight of the system by a Federal Judge named William Wayne Justice who ushered in a revamp of the Disciplinary Rules and Procedures. There was abolishment of inmate overseers called building tenders who had a virtual license to kill (or at least maim) and rules implemented that govern uses of force by guards over inmates. Even something as minor as a push or grabbing of the arm had to be reported and documented. Unit law libraries were created and expanded. Access to court rules were established. Inmates were allowed to help others with legal work (prior to this, "writ writers" were to be oppressed and suppressed). Educational opportunities were created. Medical and dental went from inmates literally pulling teeth and doing medical procedures on other inmates to the hiring of real doctors and dentists. There is virtually no area of this system that went untouched by the Ruiz case and its progeny. It also started a construction boom in Texas that lasted from 1985 to roughly 1996 or so that as the Texas prison population grew from roughly 40,000 to 150,000 currently.

Simultaneously on the streets of America, the crack epidemic swept in creating havoc. Because crack was primarily an urban epidemic, prisons were flooded with black and hispanic youngsters. The wave of crack also brought a flood of money to the dealers. So because the crack came from California, the birthplace of Crips and Bloods, those gangs were exported and transplanted all over the country, primarily to protect this flood of drug money and protect territory.

Eventually, these youngsters would meet up in prison. Kids from different "sets," different cities, but under the same color. And it was under those colors that they banded together.

Because they were street gangs, these members weren't respected by the prison gangs. The administration mistakenly assumed that because these kids were hyper violent on the street, they would be the same in prison. That wouldn't prove to be the case. At least not for a few years until the breakdown in the old racially organized prison gangs. These old archetypal structures would be done away with by something you'd never imagine would have that power or influence. Rap music.

You would think of a thousand other things before you'd come to rap music, but it's the third of the three things that changed prisons across this country. Again it was the urban nature of rap along with crack that gave rise to groups such as N.W.A., the godfathers of "Gangsta Rap," with Ice T and a couple of others telling the tale of crack, the effects it had on their community, their relationship with the police, and the rise of the "prison-industrial-complex," but our hispanic brothers were right there also. Dealing drugs, running from the cops, getting locked up, etc. The lifestyle was depicted in movies such as "Boyz in the Hood," "Colors," "Menace to Society," "Blood in Blood Out," and "American Me."

Rap music became the theme music for the later eighties and early-to-mid- nineties. The story was being told by hispanics too. Mellow Man Ace, Kid Frost, A Lighter Shade of Brown, and others. And it was because of rap that the black and hispanic kids spoke the same language. They had suffered the same treatment from the cops. Had attended the same concerts and bought the same albums. Could recite the same songs. So by the time they met up in prison, they were no longer alien life forms to each other. It was harder for the old school hardliners to sell the tropes of racial inferiority and the like. Those kids knew better.

By the time they met up in prison, the Mexicans had just as much if not more "dope-boy swagger" than the gangster-est black kid. They had the slang down pat. The mannerisms down cold and had been using the n-word all their lives with the approval of their black peers, even dating black girls and fathering their kids. But the same could be said for the other side. To the same extent hispanics had been transformed by their exposure to black culture, the black kids had been transformed also. They started sagging, wearing pants below their hips. They used bandannas, dated hispanic women, and embraced the lowrider car culture (The '64 Impala is THE GANGSTER RIDE!), which is clearly visible in the early videos of N.W.A., Dr Dre, Snoop Dog, and Tupac. This was a mutual exchange of cultures. There were and are thousands of hispanic Crips and Bloods. There are even non-racial gangs started by hispanics that blacks can join.

All this interchange was lethal to the old way of doing things, and the Texas Prison system would never be the same. Nor would California, Florida, New York prisons, or prisons anywhere have a fairly equal representation of black and hispanic inmates in the prison system.

Now what does any of this have to do with the "Demon in Hell Mentality"? I don't know. I got derailed back there, Bailey. Sorry about that. But to explain the Demon in Hell Mentality, I'll say there's a fairly common mental image of hell where there's fire, gloom, demons, and their charges in everlasting torment. In this hell, everyone is there because of something they did. No one is innocent. You are sent to hell TO BE PUNISHED. And every time a demon sees you adjusting to your torment or finding any comfort, no matter how slight, the demon runs over and pokes you in the ass with his pitchfork just to remind you that you're in hell, and there'll be no adjustment to torment. No finding of comfort. There will be only punishment.

There are prison guards that see their role as that of the role of the demons in hell I just described. If they see you greeting a friend in the hallway, they yell at you to make you disperse. Find a wire to use as an antenna for better reception for the radio out here in the sticks? That's contraband. If your family comes to visit you, he will delay telling you or turn you around because you have on personal clothes instead of state boots. He'll refuse your wife or daughter entry because he judges their pants to be too tight, shirt too low or shorts too short even though they've driven 300 miles from home for this once per year visit. Making sure I know at every turn that I'm in prison, and I'm to be punished for my crimes is all he cares about.

The program I'm currently in here allows us to send out two letters per week. They provide the envelope and stamps. You are getting mine this week. If nothing else, you'll have plenty to read.

This is therapeutic for me. I need this, Bailey. Thanks for writing to me. I truly appreciate it and look forward to your letters. Bailey, I have a request. I couldn't help but

notice the computer on your desk and think of all the things I could research if I had access to a computer. I would like to ask you if you would look up a couple of things for me and print them out and send them to me. They are a part of what I think is my "purpose" that I'm working on. But I lack access to information. In your letter, let me know if you can help. I would appreciate it.

Take care my friend and again thanks for your friendship.

Yours,
Floyd

BABYFACE

Bailey,

Hello friend. What do you mean you and your wife are not compatible? Explain please. Yes, you are very weird but I like it. A good weird lol. One of a kind is the term.

As for when we get whooped by the 'po-po,' well, all we have to do is not comply with them or simply dash them with water. They will spray us and if we continue to refuse orders, they will suit up and come in to our cell and beat the shit out of us. Also remember that inside a cell there is no cameras, so if they can get away with something, they will do it. Like grip our nuts, stick a finger in our butt, and shit like that. They obviously don't pull your pants down but they can press through your shorts hard. They do that when you're on the ground still fighting.

I thought I was going to have to fight the laws not too long ago, Bailey. You see I be in my cell, and I mind my business. Well, this black dude about 50 years old, "so-called gangster," has problems with my black homie that I talk to everyday. Well, they were talking shit to each other one day and simply because I'm friends with the young black dude, the other dude was like, "When we go to Apod and we are allowed to have group recreation you'll have to pay tax to come out."

So usually the average person would jump up and go to the cell door and start yelling back to defend their hurt pride. But I ain't say shit because one thing about me is I don't give one shit what people think, and I show not talk. So the next day he was escorted to the shower by my cell. So I finally asked him, "so what was that you was saying yesterday?" He said he was ½ cell warrioring meaning just talking shit, but he said since I never speak up that I'm basically co-signing to the trash talk (bullshit). He did what he did to sound tough in front of everybody. He thinks he will be okay talking that tough shit since nobody does anything. He thinks I'm soft. So I told his birch ass that he knows damn well I don't say none because it has nothing to do with me, but fuck all that. I'm looking for problems now. So because he is in the shower close to me has has to pass by my cell door again. He thought he was safe but I always have the metal food tray slot on my door tampered to where I can kick it open. Well I kicked it open and got ready for him to pass by. So I got a razor blade in one hand and a cup of boiling water in the other. If he is close to my door I'ma cut his stupid ass up, if he is far I'ma dash him. Well, he passed and he was too far. I threw the water, and he was hurting, but I also hit the officer . . . oops. Ol boy was still talking shit and got close, and I opened the slot, and he jumped back when I tried to reach for him. The officer was yelling at the sergeant saying go get the team. But the sergeant is cool and its too early in the morning for this shit, so he came to the door and said, "What's up with you?" I immediately told them I wasn't trying to hit his officer. I told the officer as well, and he understood, and they already knew the black dude talks a lot of shit. So all they did was take all my containers. I think the babyface had a lot to do with it too lol. But yeah I almost caught a couple charges and got my ass beat.

I know this sounds crazy, but you have to understand that not only am I in a gang, but in prison whenever somebody disrespects you you have to beat his ass if not your time will be tough because nobody respects you now. Now everybody runs you over. Believe it or not Texas prisons is pretty gangsta. Well, in Maximum security it is anyways.

Have I ever told you about my gang? You would trip on the realization that inmates run these prisons (especially gangs). Right now where I'm housed when it comes to drugs it's difficult to get a hold of, but we still get it. But in almost every unit drugs is literally everywhere! Inmates are always fucking female laws. A lot of gay shit too. Did you know that a lot of people make thousands quick and easy as an inmate? I was doing that from inside my cell but I lost it all when I lost my phone. Even you could help and get a lot of money without getting in trouble. There is no way to get in trouble. They can't stop it. But yeah prison life is crazy, Bailey.

I'ma share this photo with you. I had a copy. I usually don't feel comfortable sending valuable once in a life time captured memories, but I think I'm close enough to you to share with you. My small sis is 13 right now! That's my step father. My dad has always been there, and he has two kids with other women. Me and my brothers are from the same dad. This is my little cousin's 9th birthday.

Till next time. Take care.

Matthew

SELF-HELP

Dear Bailey,

How are you, my good friend? Miss you and think about you almost daily. Bailey, I'm going to share something with you that's a tough subject for me to speak about, but I'm comfortable with you and trust you, so I don't feel nervous nor am I concerned about how you would react to the content of this conversation. Plus, I could use your assistance in relation to locating a valuable resource I could really use.

Okay, so I know you have heard me speak a lot about the lawsuit I am working on. It's already been filed in the federal court. In a nutshell, my lawsuit is for sexual assault, sexual harassment, and for not providing me with the psychological treatment that protocol requires. I was sexual assaulted around 40 times or so in 2014 (at a different institution) by my work supervisor who I worked for in the kitchen. In case you're wondering, the defendant is a female not a male, which, by the way, is extremely uncommon for a male inmate to acknowledge that they were in fact a victim and pursue a civil litigation behind the fallout.

I guess I have a lot of mixed emotions cause there's just a lot of confusion with the whole experience, so honestly, I hardly ever talk about it to anyone cause it's like taboo anyway to talk about something like that around my peers. They don't find anything wrong with what I experienced. On the contrary, they have this outlook that "I was lucky" to have sexual interactions with a female staff. But if they were in my shoes and felt the way I felt, they would understand.

In 2015, I was interviewed by a detective about an ongoing investigation that was taking place for months (that I didn't know of previously) in regards to a lot that was coming to light about the defendant in my lawsuit and a shitload of staff she was allegedly involved in. I talked to the detective about my situation with the defendant, and let me tell you, from that time forward things have been tough with both sides (my peers as well as the administration). Peers because "How dare I cooperate with that investigation that labeled me a victim," and with the administration because they know I have a favorable lawsuit, and they feel like I got away with something and that because I'm a male, I should not have an issue with what I experienced.

To say the least, I don't have many friends, and every which way I turn, I'm getting retaliated against by the administration in one way, shape, or form, so it absolutely sucks. I keep a lot bottled up so I don't have to stress out my few loved ones who care for me.

The area of civil law is extremely complicated, but I am doing my best to litigate it on my own. The library here is extremely limited in resources, but they had a book I was using that is all about civil litigation, and I swear as soon as they figured out that said particular book was helping me prepare documents, they came and took it out of the law library, so Bailey when you have a moment, can you please jump online and look for this book:

Prisoner Self-Help Litigation Manual

And I give you my word that when I win my lawsuit, I will pay you back for it. If it's too expensive, and you just cannot do it at the moment, then can you see if that company has a physical address. If so, can you send me the physical address to that company? If you are able to purchase the book for me, and the company mails it to me, they have to let me have the book. They cannot deny it cause it's legal.

Well, Bailey. I'll wrap this up here. I hope that it was okay that I told you what I told you. Anyhow, my friend, you take care. Big hug and plenty of love being sent your way. Your friend,

Dominic!

PRUNES AND PEANUT BUTTER AND JELLY SANDWICHES

Bailey,

So so glad that you wrote to me! Pat Conroy! I read 'Prince of the Tides' back in 1988 or so and was riveted! "Savannah" reminded me so much of a very close loved one. That family went through hell!

I'm at the age now where I've ruled a lot of things out as far as pursuits and have kinda focused on the idea of PURPOSE, the question being "If I were put on this earth for a purpose, what would that purpose be? Also, is it possible to find out one's purpose? How would one go about doing so?"

I mean I've done crimes, and not all of them led to an arrest or punishment. But thankfully I've never killed or seriously harmed anyone physically. And I say that while in no way minimizing the harm done, whether financial or emotional to the victims of my crimes. I only mean to convey that my consciounce is not burdened by some truly horrendous act, and the punishment I am paying now should settle my debt to society.

I want to live differently. And more importantly, I want to make a difference. Okay, enough of that mealy mouthed stuff.

Everyone here is anticipating and dreading Christmas and the semi-annual lock down that is sure to come this month. It's where, twice a year, the entire unit of 3,400 men are locked in their cells for 24 hours a day for usually about 2 weeks until the entire unit is searched. During that time, we eat prunes, peanut butter and jelly sandwiches (which I love), and cold cuts. That's the "dreaded" part. The anticipated part is the Christmas meal. At which time we get to eat two (yes 2!) trays! One tray is a "hot tray" where there is green bean casserole, dressing, cheese biscuits, potatoes, gravy, sweet potatoes and ham. The other is a "cold tray" of sweet pickles, olives, sliced jalapenos, turkey, cheese (American), one turnover, one cookie, one slice of pumpkin pie, and one slice of cake! This was also done at Thanksgiving for which I always give thanks!

I'll close this letter by saying I wish you and yours the best. Until next time love those kids and take care of yourselves.

Yours,
Floyd Ike Williams

RIPPLE EFFECT

Bailey

Your letter to me was dated June 01 and I got it on the 11th. Because I was moved a couple of times and it bounced from each of the previous cells back to the mailroom until it got to me. Quite often guards won't ask for the inmates identifying information before giving him the mail. And SOME inmates will literally weigh the letter before they decide to give it back to the guard if it belongs to someone else. Any magazines or newspapers that are mis-delivered could be read and passed around before being returned to the guard if they returned at all!

Is your town being affected by protests, peaceful or otherwise? I think this will be different, Bailey. I mean when I saw NASCAR drivers voicing their calls for reforms/changes, THAT really struck me. And athletes that would normally stay quiet and ride this type of stuff out are out there being vocal about the status quo. I really thought that the riots and looting would drain public support for the underlying frustration, but it hasn't. And now that THAT unpleasantness is out of the way, hopefully we as a people, as a country can come to some solutions that are actually substantial and effective.

The Dale Carnegie book you sent to me a year ago is getting well used and appreciated. I hear guys telling others about that book as well as the "Compound Effect." They all love trying to explain the 1 penny doubled every day for 30 days adding up to $10 million. For a while that was a big thing with everyone trying to prove or disprove the math of that claim. But it was because of that book that you sent to me Bailey.

Talk about a ripple effect.

Please keep me in your prayers, Bailey, as you all will be in mine.

Your friend,
Floyd

IT'S BEEN CRAZY

Hi Bailey,

Things have been crazy here. A lot of drugs again, so a lot of people on meth looking like idiots. It doesn't involve me none. I watched a guy get beat up pretty bad yesterday. A guy I knew died of cancer. I saw him on the news tonight. God bless him and his family. A guy escaped from the last yard I was on. They still haven't found him. One of my OGs is in the hospital because another old guy threw boiling water on him at 3am while he was asleep. It's been crazy.
  I hope to hear from you soon.

Your friend,
Jason

CORNBREAD

Hey Bailey,

My name is Roman. I am 23 years old. I have been incarcerated for about 6 years for two aggravated robberies. I came to prison when I was 17 years old. I should be getting released in the next 30 days. I got parole. It may be tomorrow, next week, or the week after that, but I should be out there before the end of this month, unless I get in trouble. Of course I'm going to try my best to stay out of trouble, but I'm in a maximum security farm, and in a place like this, you never know what's going to happen. Things are so uncertain. The last riot in the unit was over a piece of cornbread. I know it doesn't make sense, but that's the way it is here. I was G5 for a year, that's like super high security. You don't get to come out of the cell at all. If you do come out of the cell for whatever reason like to go to the dentist or to see the doctor, you have to be in handcuffs all the time, but yeah while I was back there, I spent my time educating myself. I ordered a lot of books about different topics: real estate, investmenting, how to start your own business, clean technology, archaeology, all types of different things. That's how I have been doing my time—getting smart, stronger, bigger and faster. I am ready to come out and be successful. I ain't coming back to the pen. Stay strong and take care.

Roman Dominguez

CRASH TEST DUMMY

Hi Bailey

I hope you are well when this finds you! I was sent to another yard, and from there I was classified as minimum custody, which allowed me to start working. After becoming minimum, I was sent to a minimum custody prison where inmates work for the Nevada Department of Forestry as firefighters. I spent about 4 months there, and then I was transferred to this camp that runs a wild horse training program. For the past year, I have been here breaking wild mustangs for adoption. I have totally fallen in love with it! I'm somewhere between a cowboy and a crash test dummy.

What books have you been reading? I look forward to hearing from you.

Connor Lewis

THREE EASY PAYMENTS OF 85 CENTS

Bailey,

I want to start out by saying that I didn't sleep very well last night. I had my "pillow" confiscated which threw my comfort level off. Between coffee, discomfort, and this letter, I didn't sleep between 12:30am and 4:00am this morning. I am going to salvage the remainder of this day by tackling this letter to you.

1. Prison reform. This is a very very good thing. I would love to contribute to your efforts in any way I can. I've been in and around this place for 30+ years and have really thought about a lot of things pertaining to the system and its effects on the men and their families.

2. How long have I been incarcerated? Above I told you 30+ years. That time breaks down like this: In 1986 I was locked up and given a 4 year sentence. Because I was small (142 lbs) and scared, I over reacted to just about everything and everybody. I ended up with 5 additional years added to my sentence and I eventually did 6 years and 10 months on that 9 year sentence. I was released in July 1993. I was re-arrested in September 1993, serving 2 ½ years. Was released November 1995. I was re-arrested in October 1996 and sentenced to 5 years and did all of it. Was released October 2001, re-arrested 2002, and given a 40 year sentence. I came up for parole for the first time on that 40 year term in January 2022 after serving 20 of these 40 years. I have served 33 of my 54 years in prison. Bailey, I have never written that before. Certainly I've never told anyone that before. How could I explain that? Who would even listen to such an explanation? The numbers are staggering as I re-read it. But there it is. In black and white.

3. Your statement, "You are incredibly articulate and obviously have a good mind." It has always stabbed me in my heart to hear or read anything like that. Because how could I reconcile your opinion with the timeline above? Where would I begin to explain? I can't.

4. As for your caring about people in prison. That is a beautiful thing, Bailey. And not simply because I'm on the receiving end of your letters. I believe that caring speaks volumes about your kindness and passion for people. It goes hand in hand with your love for those children. It's not only respectable, but it's also honorable. And I appreciate you for it.

5. "... people who appreciate my letters and need them." That's me! I didn't tell you this before, but I bought your address. I paid 85¢ for it. The guy, I forgot his name, was complaining about how long it took for you to respond to his letter, and I asked for your info. Sight unseen. But once he saw me interested, he charged me a packet of mackerel filets worth 85 cents. Does that sound weird? If this was the NFL, it would be the equivalent of the deal that sent Hershel Walker from the Dallas Cowboys to the Minnesota Vikings. The Cowboys got in return players and draft picks that had them winning the Super Bowl three times in the next 6 years! And to make it even crazier, it took me almost 3 months to pay the mackerel filet! So there!

6. When you wrote in your last letter that you'd sent a book, or more specifically "one of my all-time favorite books." I thought you were referring to the "Blueprint For Happiness" post by Tony Robbins that you'd included with your letter. I wouldn't receive the Darren Hardy book until the following night. Bailey that was a very nice gesture, sending that book. Giving me something that could potentially change my life. That is truly nice. I don't want to sound corny or trite

or . . . anything else. I just want to say thank you. I've done this time by myself for all these years.

It was the idea that no one would miss me. That I wasn't leaving anyone behind that made this/these incarcerations . . . less bad from my vantage point. It was just me. But then before she died, my mother started writing to me and that was like a ray of light into this darkness I'd enveloped myself in. Then, she passed away a few years later in 2013. The clouds moved in again. But, "for three easy payments" of 85 cents, I get Bailey as a pen-pal! And the sun shines again. So yeah, Bailey, your letters, your time, your gift of this book are truly appreciated. Truly a ray of sunlight in this darkness.

7. Bailey, this and every prison ever created is like an island of broken toys. Everyone here is missing something that would make them "normal." But we are all convinced that we're normal and everyone else is broken. In fact, we revel in our brokenness. In our anti-normalness. But because when we only compare ourselves to other broken toys, we seem normal by comparison. The truly normal people, who go to work each day and raise their children and invest in those children with morals and social skills we lack, they are the weirdos. They are the ones who've never "really lived." As a result of this view of ourselves, we spend a tremendous amount of time in frivolous talk, activities, and thinking. You'd be surprised. You would be astonished and/or disappointed. We have women that work here as guards. They do the same job as male guards. And overwhelmingly, these women are shocked at how we, as men, spend our days. And it's not "the system"—it's us. We're broken, and no matter how many programs, classes, or courses are implemented, this will not change. Nothing will change for a man until he tires of boyishness and takes on manhood. And that takes time. Cutting sentences won't help; scholarships won't help; family involvement won't help. All that stuff will only be useful if and when that guy decides to put aside boyishness and embrace manhood.

I can't begin to tell you the number of 20, 30, 40, and 50 year olds who are in a prolonged state of adolescence. Have you heard about how they used to capture monkeys? They would hollow out a log or a part of a log and leave a small hole. They would put candy in the hollowed out part and wait for the monkey to reach inside for the candy. Because the hole was only large enough to accommodate an open hand, the monkeys couldn't extract their hands once they grabbed the candy. The hunters could literally walk up and grab the monkeys because the monkeys wouldn't let go of the candy. That's how many prisoners are. We can't move forward because we won't let go of adolescence. Literally trapped in our childhood.

All we wanted as kids was to be grown ups. To be free. To be men. But all we knew were the superficial aspects of manhood. A car, money, sex, no one telling us what to do. But as soon as we get control of our lives we run into a ditch. Convinced it was just a fluke, we try again. Again the ditch. Prison officials believe that our problem is that we skipped too many steps in development, so the solution is to go back and complete these missed steps. Clean your room! Pull up your pants! Go to school! No horseplay! Stop playing with yourself! All the things you thought of as worthless and a waste of time. Go back and learn those things. And the worst thing is that you're being treated like a child! You're being yelled at, often by someone much younger than yourself. And many times by a woman (it's worse when women use the "mom tone" to yell at you). Drives us crazy! We live in a prolonged state of adolescence. A prolonged state of play with an aversion to responsibility. The whole gang problem is simply an adult way of playing "cowboys and indians" or "cops and robbers." A prolonged state of play. The women we married or lived with were simply moms. They washed our clothes, cleaned our rooms, cooked our food, and everything else our moms did when we were young. And since having sex with one's mom is taboo, we go out and have sex outside our relationship. Only have sex with "mom" when we had to. And too many women enabled us in this, refusing to hold us accountable and demand more from us. So here we sit. Like kids forced to take a time out. We can't wait to go back 'outside' and play with our friends and chase girls.

All the time we were grounded, did we actually think about what we'd done wrong that got us 'grounded' in the first place? No. We were too busy watching the clock or calendar for the next opportunity to play again. The only thing that will change this is the time and introspection and the realization that life has passed you by. And all the girls you like are your children's age. You also realize that one more grounding and you will most likely die in that corner.

If I re-read this, I'm sure I'll tear it up. To prevent that, I'll forgo the re-read and send it. For better or worse, here it is. Thank you for your time, your caring, and your friendship. Peace to you and your family.

Floyd

EVERYTHING COUNTS

Hey friend,

You may be my best friend. I mean over all your actions speak louder than your words. Guess what? My b-day is on the 21st of this month. I'm going to be 27. Only thing bad about that is I gotta make a cake out of cookies and pastries. On another note, you know me being 27 brought about me questioning myself as far as am I there mentally? I took inventory and realized I'm at a mature level. I realize I'm really well rounded up top. I mean, I know I got my priorities straight. I know I'm wise enough not to find myself in a position that I wouldn't want to be in. I just gotta make it home, Bailey.

Speaking of making it home, I'm asking you for a big favor. Do you mind writing to the parole board on my behalf just as a friend to let them know how you may feel about me as a person, giving them a reason to let me make it home? Many times the reason people don't make parole is just because of the lack of a support system, and some people, including my own family, don't understand how far a letter or a simple phone call would go on a person's behalf. But if you would do this, I would highly appreciate it. Everything counts. I see parole next month. I hope to hear from you soon take care.

Nathaniel Townsend

REMEMBERED FOR BEING GOOD

Bailey

As you can see, I was transferred to another unit, so it takes 2 weeks to follow me. They take their sweet time to give or send our mail. They are not supposed to do that, but as much as we report it, we can't do much. They lie to cover their backs.

As for the status on me. Long story short, I was betrayed by the only person I thought I had love and trust for. Life and its curve balls, huh? I was on my way to him and was caught at the destination with a 8-inch shank. Immediately, I was placed in segregation.

Now let me tell you a lil bit about segregation if you are not already familiar. In seg, we get placed by ourselves in a room that is as small and as wide as the span of your arms if not just a few inches smaller. For 90 days we have no commissary or radio. So I'm in a cell that is quiet day and night. I have to survive on what the state provides. When I recently got here, I was stressing so hard I was losing it. I had a lot going on. I came to the realization that the female I love is not exactly on the same page, and I was over here thinking I had someone who cared for years. Since I got locked up, everybody who owed me decided to not give me my money since I'ma get shipped anyways. So I lost close to $5,000.

It was just too much, Bailey. I was in a small cell (still am) with little to occupy my mind. I take pills for depression now. Well, I'm supposed to. Whenever they do let me out for whatever, I have to be handcuffed before I come out. When I'm out, I have to be held by two officers, and as I leave, there is a glass as big as the door that slides. The purpose of that is when I'm being escorted, it is used to cover me from getting speared or dashed with boiling water or shit.

I'm in a whole different world, and it's depressing as fuck. I was doing good, and I was indulging myself in the right things. I was making money so fast and easy. But I guess I will bounce back.

I had bought this book. I forgot the name of the book, but it was just recently published. He is a billionaire, and he shares his life story. He gives some awesome insights on ways to go about running a business. Now I have a better understanding of things. We have to ask ourselves the right questions to figure out what people want.

The plan is to excel in one business and to invest and learn about other types of assets so I have money coming in. This is what that guy from the book does, but he's on his best shit.

I don't know, Bailey, but my goals and priorities are not the same. You play a part in it as well. I appreciate you, Bailey. There are a lot of people who have the knowledge but lack motivation and desire and are content to feel secure where they are. But as for me, I will do something about my destiny. I will indulge myself with what I'm trying to pursue. I want to own a building in Houston and help people. I want to pass on and be remembered for being good. I know you do as well, and this is why I feel you are a good friend to be around with. If you was to hang with me, you would see that I'm always gonna look hood AF. Lol. This is my culture, Bailey. But that will trick people because my mind is targeting prosperity. Not what people would expect from my appearance.

Enough about me.

Take care and God bless you. I appreciate you and the love and concern you have shown me. I wish I could give you a gift.
Your friend,
Matthew N.

BURNT

Dear Bai,

I just got out of the box. They threw me under the pen. I, no joke, did 6 months in the box. They gave me 180 for allegedly running a drug ring. Lol. They said I was introducing contraband to the prison. They had no evidence. I got conspiracy. Drug possession and conspiracy distribution. In a single cell for 180 days. Fml. Everybody talks to me because they know I keep things to myself. Everybody needs an ear!

They do have a library, but it is small. You can't physically see the books. They make you request a book, if they have it they have it. If not, your burnt. My days are truthfully full of drama. Everytime there is an issue, I'm at yard and the gang members have to talk to me to do anything. There are more independent blacks than gang members. Gang members set the tempo. I decide if the independent blacks get in the mix or not. Too much drama, but I'm the perfect guy. Sometimes you have to lace up and attack the problem to establish stipulations amongst people. All that aside just know:

Love can cure anything. Even the worst evil.

Damien Lanson

THANKFUL

Dear Bailey,

I turned 40 years old April 23rd. I'm getting old, girl! Birthdays are bittersweet for me as this is my 22nd birthday straight while locked up, and well, of course, you can imagine it sucks to be in such a dark, sadistic place on what is supposed to be a bright day. So the sweet comes in where that little cozy place in my heart allows me to dance no matter the madness and ugliness that surrounds me. In spite of conditions and circumstances, I'm able to breathe, smile, and be thankful for the experience of another birthday.

Your friend, Floyd

SOLITUDE

Bailey

Hey, my sweet friend. Well I'm writing to update you on my new location! I've been transferred to a psych program that lasts 7 months or so. Once completed, I will be released from solitary! Wish me luck because I seem to like to bend the rules at times. Yolo, gang! I could have joined other programs, but this is the fastest way to get out. What's crazy is that there's people here who throw their doodoo at you! I bet you wasn't expecting that, huh? Some people if you get into it with them, they will threaten you saying, "I'mma shit you down *********!" And others will do it because they are bored. Crazy huh? That's solitude for yuh. Especially at a psych program. And you know what else though? Man . . . I walked to my new cell, and the previous "resident" was either crazy or dirty. Maybe even both, but there were mice turds everywhere, unknown liquids on the floor, gnats everywhere, roaches, and it was just a complete mess. I got it clean though. I hate sitting around when it ain't clean and organized. How is the fam? Well, take care and God bless y'all.

Your homeboy,
Matthew Navarro

DESPERATE

Dear Bailey

Don't think I was avoiding you. I just got done doing 180 days in the hole and didn't have your address. I've been going through it. I feel comfortable sharing what I'm going to share with you. I have been bestfriends with someone for 5 years. Him and I met in county jail. We have naturally always just had an understanding of each other. I recently, as in about a year ago, sat him down and broke down to him. I told him I loved him in a way I havent loved another male. The feeling was mutual. He confessed he loved me more than his baby mom. All of it blew me away. This whole time we have been in the same cell 5 times and have kept it inside.

We got the chance to cell up and another person said when they walked by they saw something. That person told everybody, and all the blacks started talking on the low about the situation, and then my bros found out. Since he is a gang member the rules apply different to him. It became an issue, so I got violent and went to the hole for 6 months. Now I'm back out and I got to deal with this. Half of me is so in love with him I don't care who knows . . . Then the other half has to think about his safety. I can't let him get hurt.

I have been down 5 years and haven't known my sexuality. People have made passes I just haven't been sure. I'm still not sure. All I know is I've never loved a female like this. I write him poems. We deliver scripts all day. Right now the units are all on lockdown, so I haven't been able to see him because of this virus situation. I'm not sure what to do. I'm so desperate to see him. I've never felt like this over any person before. Now people assume they know what's going on between him and I, but they have no clue. It sucks, and I can't talk to anyone about it. Nobody in my family or anyone for that part knows but you. I guess I wrote you because I feel you won't judge me because if you judged me you would have not wrote me.

All this shit sucks. Everybody, well 80% of people, changed up on me and are treating me like I'm just a horrible person not even knowing if the rumors are true. It's so dumb. I'm just mad I can't be with my bro. I'm not going to go too deep. I'm not trying to make you feel uncomfortable about it. I could write 100 pages on it. Lol. I have found I'm codependent on him for certain emotions. I hate it, but I can't control it. He gets out in 8 months though. I'm low-key devastated. But I can't fight the facts, I can only face them . . . Get at me ASAP.

Damien Lanson

THE CLIMATE OF OUR COUNTRY

Hey Bailey,

I'm good, been building myself and recently went through a spiritual growth causing a mental shift. I'm seeing things in a new way. I'm excited about this new chapter.

So, in the climate of our country right now, how do you talk to your kids about racism, or race in general? I know that you being so open minded and having an open heart (If I'm not proof of that, black with dreadlocks and tattoos in prison, I don't know what more evidence is needed), there is probably no hate in your home, but with that said, I don't know what the level of diversity is there.

You're a white woman (you're more than just a white woman to me but generally speaking), and I'm an African-American man, but we have been able to create a sort of bond just through pen and paper, never actually seeing each other in person. We have great conversations, and we connect, which is a beautiful thing. I say bless this relationship for what it is.

Speaking of relationships, I am conflicted about how I feel when it comes to being in one. Because of my legal situation, I don't want to be a burden. It wouldn't be fair to her. Plus, honestly, I'm a bit scared of women, because all they have to do is say something happened, and the courts will believe her because they would rather be wrong and put an innocent man in prison just to save face than be wrong and take the chance of letting a guilty man go. So I feel if it happened to me once, it'll be easier for it to happen again, so bottom line, I'm afraid to open myself to a woman again.

Thank you for an amazing letter. Once again, your letters always seem to show up right on time. Glad to hear you're doing well and hope to hear from you soon.

*Your friend,
Dale Walker*

ONCE A WEEK

Bailey,

I hope you and your family have been well and full of joy. As for me, I haven't been so well lately. Since January the 17th, I have been placed in segregation and shipped to another unit. As you already knew, I was able to do more than the ordinary prisoner. I was able to communicate with my family and have money stacked up in the bank. Thanks to you and them awesome books and words you shared with me, I have also changed my way of thinking and how I choose to indulge myself. I was doing real good, B. But then I was jacked by someone I trusted. I never trusted no one, and the day I do, I get betrayed. I lost my connection and my money.

I was caught with a shank heading toward the dude who betrayed me, and that's how I got segregated. My rights were read to me, and I will be in a small cell for maybe 3 years. If you stretch both your arms, the cell is that small. I am suffering from depression, and people commit suicide at least once a week. The mail is supposed to take 3 days to get to where I'm writing and 3 back. But it actually takes 10 days to get there and 10 days back. They just barely started feeding us. They were feeding us like we were kids. I lost a lot of weight. I'm not allowed to have commissary nor a radio. So I'm in a quiet room everyday. You are the only pen-pal I wanna write because you are a productive person who has helped me. Any powerful books you have read lately? I tried ordering this book called The Great Book of Political Thinkers. But it was denied. I like that Tony Robbins Awaken the Giant Within. I always re-read it because it helps me keep my way of thinking fresh.

Believe it or not, I know how to make something out of nothing now. I know how to convince and use my mind and mouth. I know how to locate your wants and needs and come in. I do that here with who I see as an asset. I learned how to make money many different ways and how to invest. And what I wanna do. I learned to try my best to be righteous and lead with integrity. I just stress because I love too much and I don't trust no one no more. I have trust issues. I'mma end it right here. I will be ok. I always am. I never stop swinging. Whatever is on your mind, I'm here also.

Your friend,
Matthew Navarro

THE MAIN TOPIC IS LIFE

Dear Bailey,

Thank you for listening to my story. Once I found out about you and the research you do to help troubled kids, I felt responsible to help your cause, to share my own troubled life story so that people can learn from my mistakes and not follow my footsteps. I wouldn't wish my prison sentence on my worst enemy.

This Christmas I will be gone for a total of 9 years. I am convicted of Agg. Assault on Public Servant w/ deadly weapon (ink pen) 50-year sentence, agg. Robbery x2, and another agg. Robbery x2, in which I have been given two 40-year sentences. All run together, so the 50 year sentence is really all I have. I have to do half to come up for parole (25 years, 16 left).

If I would have had help as a child I do believe I wouldn't be here now because I had no one to talk to, no one to really understand the way I was feeling. I wanted to go wherever my mother went, but at the same time I knew it was wrong. Most of all I wish I had a counselor to consult with at that time. It's crazy you say that about your problem with depression. Me and another million inmates struggle with the same problem. Just like you, we pick up reading habits to occupy our minds. It is a healthy habit indeed.

I had to face my problems, accept the truth about my mother and realize that I will never get answers to the questions I have. With that being said, I had to let it go. That's very hard for men to do. But I did it. I've overcome that part of my life. Now, I'm asking God for a second chance to get out sooner so I'll have a better opportunity at living life happy and peaceful.

Being locked up is hard, Bailey, but it's something I have to accept as a man because of the mistakes I made when I was younger. Believe it or not, Bailey, prison is like college, and the main topic is life. You learn all there is about it because with all the other inmates around you, you get to see life from other inmate's perspectives. It's crazy to explain but just by being quiet and observing another's actions, character, and personality, you can discover what type of person they are. But prison is also hell on earth. You have your good days, but most days are hell. The officers and some inmates keep drama going. I've been gone so long, I just stay out of known drama queens' ways! Most of all, prison makes an individual very bright. In 2009, there's no way I would have even spoken have the proper words in this letter. If we went out to eat at an expensive restaurant in 2009, you would have been embarrassed to even know such a person who speaks like I did then. I still speak to homeboys from the street but it's a firm way I speak.

I will be 29 years old this Friday. I am too old to be ignorant any more. I must be genuine for the rest of my days. Yes, I still talk to my sisters, but I haven't spoken to the oldest in over a year now. I talk to the youngest very often. I would send you a picture of me, but I haven't had a visit since 2013. I will be looking forward to getting a letter from you. Take care, and I hope to hear from you soon.

*Yours truly,
Marques Jr.*

THIS PRISON HAS A PSYCH WARD

Dear Bailey,

I hope life has been treating you well. Me, on the other hand, its been so much going on in my life that I attempted suicide. I'm still in prison, but this prison has a psych ward. It's so much to speak on. I just really hope you will respond to me and let me know that you are still around for me and let me know what's going on in your life. I miss our corresponding so please write me back asap.

Peace and love,
Quintavius

NO ONE

Bailey,

Hopefully my letter don't bring you hurt. Right now I'm in the hole for fighting. I lost my cousin just this past week. She was 24 and 7 months pregnant. My head is so fucked up right now. I have no one to talk to. Feels like someone stabbed me in the heart a million times. I really feel like my life doesn't get better at all. There's only so much I can take, Bailey. I've been crying to fucking much it hurts. My life is past the lowest point right now. I'm full of pain and anger, depressed. Me and her were close. You don't want to hear about my painful life. You're too focused on your own great life, huh? I have it too hard right now, Bailey. I have no one! Please send me another book. Maybe that will help a little? How's your life right now? Good, huh? Bailey, I would love to make you mine, but like you said, you have a life. It's so fucked up that I can't even find love. Why keep trying? There's so much wrong with me right now and no one here for me. Bailey, please tell me what to do. Tell me something. Are you in love, Bailey? I want to be in love, free from marriage. Well, I hope everything is the best with you, Bailey.

Love,
Simon Collins (AKA Lost Man)

HAVEN'T CRIED SINCE 2014

Hey Bailey,

I wanted to wish you the best Christmas ever. I'm happy I finally have someone to write for the holidays. I wrote my babies, but their mom probably won't let them write me. I have never had a visit in here. I am literally the kindest, most loving person you will ever meet. I am so confused why nobody tries to contact me. Out of all the friends I thought I had. You'll be surprised at who your friends really are. So far, you are the best friend I've ever had. I'm getting a tattoo of your name on me for you being here for me through the hardest part of my life.

You know the closer I am to getting out, I get a little nervous. I don't know if I'm doubting myself or what. I'm scared. Scared my babies won't want to see me. I feel like leaving Arizona is best for me. But I don't know where I would go. I've never left Arizona. I don't want to go back to prison. I really am a great daddy when I'm not in prison. If you were to ask any acquaintance of mine what they think of me as a person, I promise you would hear nothing but great things. I just don't get why not one person has even tried to reach me.

Do you cry? I haven't cried since 2014. Is that normal? I know I'll cry when or if I see my babies. You lose a lot of it, not all of your emotions, in here. You can't show emotions in this place. I am a very unique person because I am a survivor in here and on the street. I am living with murderers every day. One bed away I live next to a guy in here for murder. Would you be able to sleep next to someone who killed a person? And I'm talking bare hands in cold blood. I've seen people get killed in prison. Crazy, huh?

You are always in my prayers and dreams.

Your friend,
Jason

YOUR CHAPERONE

While sleeping one night I had a dream. It left a tale to tell.
I dreamed I saw an angel, and she wasn't looking well.
Her body was bruised and battered, her wings ripped and torn.
I saw that she could barely walk. She was tired, weary and worn.
I walked over to her and said, "Angel, but how can this be?"
She looked back at me and tried to smile, then said these words to me . . .
"I'm your guardian angel, quite a job as you can see.
You've lived a very hard life, with that you must agree.
You've broken laws and hearts, and what you see, you've done to me.
These bruises are from shielding you, and each day I do my best still.
The drugs you've used so recklessly, I've often paid the bill.
My wings you see are ripped and torn, a noble badge I bare.
Countless times they've shielded you, though you were unaware.
Yes, every mark has its story of pain and danger I've destroyed.
You've made me wish, more than once, that I was unemployed.
If you would only embrace life, and choose to do good on your own,
it would end the pain of suffering that goes with being your chaperone.
I will always be there to watch over you until my strength finally fails.

*As for when that will be? All I can say is I'm getting
   old and frail."*
*When I awoke, I thought about my dream, and how
   much she cared.*
*Then I looked around my prison cell, and my heart
   sank in despair.*
*As I sat there, thought and wondered, "Why should I
   even try?"*
*Suddenly the air around me rushed by, from beating
   wings,*
and I thought I heard an angel cry.

By Dominic Sanchez

MAIL CALL

Bailey,

Every night the officer walks into the pod with a bag of sorted mail and inmates gather around the table. Because the mail is called out numerically, by cell number or bunk number, many inmates simultaneously dread and anticipate the approach of their number. It's actually better if, for example, I'm in 6 cell and the officer to gets to 4 then jumps to 7, 8 or 9 because that means not just me but ALL the inmates in 6 cell, 7 cell, 8 cell and 9 cell got no mail! And they all have to take the "walk of shame" away from the table. I solved that long ago by simply appearing to be engrossed in some task during the calling of mail. It has served me well for the past decade or so.

Bailey, you asked me the question that I dread the most. Why have I been in and out of prison so much? What could I say that wouldn't sound at least somewhat self- serving and totally inadequate as an explanation? I can only say that whatever you "see" in these missives from me to you is actually a result of my time spent in this prison. I would never have had the time nor the inclination to study what I have for as long as I have without all this time spent on the sideline of life, Bailey. And more importantly, I wouldn't have the potential to be effective in reaching people and actually finishing this life on a high note had it not been for this 30+ year detour in my life.

I realize this doesn't begin to address the "why," but I have to focus on the result of the journey. The "why" would be littered with phrases like "low self-esteem," "abuse," "self- hatred," and many such phrases. But it would all come down to simply a series of extraordinarily stupid choices that I made when I didn't have to. And every time I would be so socially inept that I would draw negative attention to myself. Returning to prison would put me further behind "the times" when I eventually got out again. And it was just a vicious cycle.

The difference is that I've actually "grown into" my personality. My way of thinking, my way of talking, my way of interpersonal contact is expected from a person my current age. But it was hard being this person at twenty. Even at thirty. At least my view of myself told me so.

I am for the first time in my life comfortable in my skin, comfortable with my skill set, embracing who I am, and actually view the path my life has taken as preparation for a strong finish.

Floyd

FACTS ABOUT PRISON LIFE

In 2019, suicide accounted for 8 percent of deaths in state and federal prisons and 30 percent of death in local jails.[19] One study found that 41 percent of these suicides happened in people who were currently or had recently been in solitary confinement, which exacerbates symptoms of mental illness.[20]

"Alabama's prisons are the most violent in the nation. The U.S. Department of Justice found in a statewide investigation that Alabama routinely violates the constitutional rights of people in its prisons, where homicide and sexual abuse is common, knives and dangerous drugs are rampant, and incarcerated people are extorted, threatened, stabbed, raped, and even tied up for days without guards noticing."[21] —Equal Justice Initiative

1 in 5 African Americans in prison is serving a life sentence.[22]

The United States stands alone as the only nation that sentences people to life without parole for crimes committed before turning 18.[23]

AFTER PRISON

When a person who has been in prison is released back to society, back to their families and everything that has made them who they are, we strip them of every opportunity to succeed. Any chance they had at finding their way, anything good they found in themselves during their prison sentence—gratitude, self-awareness, maturity—often fades because there are so few opportunities for success upon release.

It is miserable to know a person can spend years in prison waiting for the day they get released, holding onto that sliver of hope that things will be different, that they will be different, but when that day comes, they find themselves walking out the door with nowhere to go and little to no opportunity to create the secure life they dreamed about during their prison sentence. Met with roadblock after roadblock, some people find work in factories or warehouses that allow for little to no human contact, but the reality is, most people who leave prison have an extremely challenging time getting a job.

There is a stigma around felons that follows them everywhere. We want people to emerge from prison and become productive members of society. We do not take action on this sentiment with rehabilitation in prison nor do we allow for opportunities upon release that would encourage successful reintegration. This is a system created on the foundation of fear. We are scared of anyone who can't keep themselves in line because of trauma, mental illness, teenage hormones, or anything else that leads people to commit crimes. So, we lock these people away, avoid even the thought of them, and once we have to release them, we push them out of society every chance we get.

If you have ever filled out a job application, you have seen the questions that ask about criminal background. This little box that felons are required to check prevents them not only from getting a job but from volunteering, going to their child's school, getting into housing, and receiving benefits that would give them and their family the ability to survive while they try to find the one person in their city willing to hire them.

When I was growing up, it was hard for my mom to find a job and housing we could afford. When we moved, we never once got a U-Haul. My mom and I tried to keep my baby brother occupied while we packed what we could into a car. Everything else was left there or given away. On the way to our new home, we slept in the backseat in a Walmart parking lot. We would arrive, start over, and hope for the best, but we were never stable for long. My mom has two Masters' degrees. If it was that hard for us, I can't imagine how hard finding a job and a place to live would be for someone after a prison sentence.

The most pressing thing I hear from my pen pals is how badly they want to change their lives and the fear that creating change will not be possible if they go home. When these people become involved in gangs, whether they grew up in a family of gang members or joined as a young person, they return home with everyone expecting them to join in on all the battles the gang is currently fighting. It is a brotherhood, and loyalty is of the utmost importance. If you no longer wish to comply, to partake in what's important to that brotherhood, you broke their trust, and life could be very dangerous for you. To escape that life, people in this situation would need to relocate and often cut out members of their own family. Considering how hard it is for people to get jobs, housing, and benefits after prison, needing to move away from home, often the only place they have upon release, seems unrealistic.

Still, the men I write have hope. They dream of opening businesses, starting non-profit organizations, and being family men—the fathers they never had. They dream of a better life. In the past, we have excluded huge portions of the population from being able to better their lives and build the American dream, and this has been detrimental to society at large. Historically, if you were considered "less," you had no voice. This is what's happening to prisoners and felons today. These people have the desire to learn, to improve, and to be great contributors to our world.

They are being left out when by giving them opportunity and a voice, our country could put a halt to the tremendous levels of criminal activity and incarceration we see today.

When people who have been put in prison receive opportunities for empowerment, the results are remarkable. The docuseries *College Behind Bars* had a profound impact on me. I took notes the entire time and sent the trailer to all of my friends. Everything I knew to be true about the potential of American people who have been put in prison was confirmed. We do so little to rehabilitate, but when we do give these people a chance, they jump at the opportunity for a better life. In fact, people in prison shown in this docuseries worked harder than any person I know including myself.

As the film opens with footage of a prison in New York, we hear these words: "I've been incarcerated for 13 years and from my experience I can tell you prison is here to punish us. Is here to warehouse us. But it's not about rehabilitating. It's not about creating productive beings."[1]

A small group of men and women from prisons in New York are given the chance to earn a bachelor's degree during their incarceration. Teachers from elite universities stepped up to provide the best education possible for these men and women, which meant enforcing rigorous standards. Those given a chance were the best students their teachers had ever seen. They came more prepared and ready to learn than anyone would expect of a high-achieving student in America.

The incarcerated students at Bard College were able to attend school *in-person*. A small section of the prison was dedicated to education. Anyone who has taken college classes online and in-person knows there is a huge difference. Many people in prison do not have the option for even online classes and, when earning a GED or certificate, take classes via mail correspondence. By having an in-person school with highly-educated college professors, Bard set these people up for success. They rose to the challenge and achieved not only the completion of degrees but the ability to learn and compete at a high level. Just one example of their great achievements is shown when the students on Bard's debate team faced Harvard University and won.[2]

They gained confidence, skills, and were able to get out of prison and get good jobs, many of which were in non-profit sectors. Recidivism rates at this prison are over 50%, but among Bard College graduates, it drops to 4%.[3]

This same level of excellence has been what I have witnessed in my pen pals. If I send a book or an article, it gets read over and over and shared with twenty other men. A poem will be studied, analyzed, and returned with a detailed reflection far deeper than anything I considered. A workbook I sent from a Tony Robbins event was received with enormous gratitude. I believe I sent workbooks to about eighteen men, and everyone who received one dedicated themselves to completing every question and working to implement what they learned. I bet Tony Robbins himself would say it is rare to see that kind of initiative.

Anyone in prison will tell you there are a lot of people in prison who make up excuses for why it's not their fault they are in prison. There is definitely an awareness among people in prison concerning the need for personal responsibility. Personal responsibility is key. I do not deny that. I just think we as a nation could do better to support the many prisoners who do take full personal responsibility and are striving to live their best lives. I also believe that if inmates were given a chance at an education, it could open their eyes to their own potential, as education does for everyone who embraces it.

The students in *College Behind Bars* proved that education in prisons is worth it. As my pen pals prepare to come home, I hear about the deep reflection, the intensive reading, the attempts at going to school and getting a GED or a certificate that will open up their opportunities. These tasks are notable in normal society. In prison, they are so much harder to accomplish but people go after them with enormous determination. What one person will do to complete a GED or CDL certificate in prison is amazing. One of my pen pals asked his mom to go to the DMV and read him information over the phone about how to get a CDL. In prison, you have to get creative.

We know that as education levels increase, crime levels decrease.[4] The 4% recidivism rates at Bard's prison college is one of many instances offering proof. The dreams and goals shared with me over years of letters have been very diverse ranging from starting a grill-making business to being a children's author. We need to offer high-quality education and training programs in-person in every prison in the United States. This one change would not only change crime and incarceration in America, it would take a massive population of 2 million people who fell into a life of crime and turn them into productive citizens. I say this with such decisiveness because I am confident in the outcome.

The only reason we have not made this change is indifference. Implementing opportunities for dreams to be realized after prison—businesses started, education earned, and jobs obtained—we could save millions of lives and, I believe, improve the direction of the United States. I understand some folks have no desire to invest in the lives of criminals. However, if we step back and look at the situation logically, not introducing education and opportunities for growth doesn't make a lot of sense. The people who make up our nation's enormous prison population (currently around 2 million people) have dreams and goals, and we would do well to cease stripping them of opportunity and encourage pathways to success.

DAYDREAMING

Dear Bailey,

What's up girl? I did get your email and double letter in one envelope—Thanks for writing, as always, I love hearing from you. The photos were absolutely gorgeous off the internet, especially that bedroom that had the rock wall and the water visible through the glass on the ceiling.

You're absolutely right that it's important to dream. Putting myself in a state of daydreaming has been my medicine countless times throughout the years and has really allowed me to push through some dark moments! Especially during my last break-up, mind you it was not just "some break up" or your typical prison relationship, which are usually one-sided. I genuinely loved this girl. She was absolutely perfect, and I wanted nothing more than to be with her, complete her, and love her. She was 13 years older than me, and I was with her from 2004 to 2015 (11 years). She just couldn't do it anymore. I was crushed but held my head up and embraced her moving on cause when all was said and done, she gave me 11 years of her life and I was extremely blessed to have been part of her life for those 11 years. You just don't hear of prison relationships lasting anywhere near that amount of time.

I've said that to say that after she said she could not do it anymore, I day dreamed of that woman all the time, and although during moments of joy, it literally felt like a surgeon was holding my heart and applying pressure to it almost in a suffocating way. It was painful, but the sweet thoughts of her trumped the pain in the end. Even speaking it to you now makes my eyes puddle up a bit cause I still love that girl. So yeah, Bailey, daydreaming moves mountains in here.

I will talk to you more later. Take care, teammate! Sendin' you a strong hug and lots of love.

*From your friend,
Dominic*

BEING THE REASON

Bailey

Thank you. Yes, I have a lot of dreams and I try to make them as realistic as possible. Italy looks amazing. I want to take my girl there on a romantic trip.

All my business ideas are something I'm really interested in, like I won't ever get tired of what I do. It'll never be about the money. It will be about bringing people together and making them happy.

Having kids is gonna make my life complete. This is when I'll become the happiest. I know they're expensive, that's why I have to have my girl to be on the same page as me. So we can build up together as one. And that's what I hope for, to give my kids the attention they need and want.

I would like to have a positive impact on people's life and contribute by individually helping people in need. Like give people a restart that they need. My main focus is to prevent kids from selling drugs, joining gangs, and shooting and killing people. I want to give them an early opportunity to work on having career or working on skill sets. And be able to teach them and educate them on stuff the schools can't teach them about. That's the whole purpose of my recreational center for kids. My dream is to give them a fair opportunity to become successful in life, and me being the reason for it.

Speak to you soon.
Deion Robinson

I WANT TO FIND LOVE.

Bailey

Hey player! It made my day—highlight of the week to get an unexpected letter with your handwriting on it. You came through when I least expected it. You are definitely awesome for that.

The new facility could be much worse, but that's not what has me upset. I am just frustrated that I am stuck here for at least another year. I am so bored. I am not allowed to have any books or magazines. So all I do is write, a lot, and workout, and that's about it. I am trying to get a pencil to redo your portrait, but that's not going to happen. So, I plan on learning to use ink as a medium. If you don't get your portrait by New Year's, then it's not going well.

Sometimes I think about what I really want in life, especially for the future ahead of me. You know? My path is the road less traveled. I am grateful that I have nothing.

Because by having nothing, I am able to truly appreciate something that is very powerful: the power of thought. Pondering and deliberating. Planning. The reason I appreciate my time is because I have to really sit back and think. Because I might otherwise have never had the opportunity to actually open my mind to every aspect of things that I realize are now important to me.

If I never would have come to prison, I would have been on the same foolish path I was on. I don't want to be angry and miserable like so many people that I see everyday. I want to get a higher education. I want to own my own home, my own vehicles. I want to find love as well. I want to have a family of my own. I want to do so much. I want to travel.

I'm a dreamer.

Long ago, my mother used to sell A LOT of drugs. And she always had her "runners." They were like my big brothers in a way. And my body guards sometimes. This was before the law built a massive case against my mother, which ultimately sent her to prison. This was during the early 2000s. When she "fell," I was around 11, 12 years old.

I'm not just "preachin" jail talk. I seriously am done. I need positive people in my life that share common goals or are like-minded individuals. By the time I get paroled, if I go back to the same people, then all this time I spent would be for nothing. Fuck that. I am done. There is so much more to live and experience. There is more to life than being a badass or a drug addict, wasting away in a heartless prison. I want to chase my dream.

Keep your head up. Stay true to yourself and those who make you feel loved and laughing and cheerful, because those are the ones who truly matter most.

Loyalty always,
Izaak Shunk

I'M NOT COMING BACK FOR NO ONE

Dear Bailey,

It means a lot to me that you still care enough to write me. I'm not sure where to start, but a while ago I basically lost everything. While I was at work, my cellmate was transferring to another facility. In the process, he packed all of his property and also packed a lot of my things as if they were his own—new clothing, face towels, socks, underwear, t-shirts, body towels, my family pictures. Many of the pictures are gone. Letters you wrote me were also missing. I no longer have your pictures. The Tony Robbins book you sent me is gone. All of these material things that would mean something to anyone in my position were stolen from my commissary, my song lyrics gone.

But on top of this, one of my old close friends—someone I slept in the same bed with, someone I called my brother, we wore each others clothes, called each others mom's "mom"—is one of the men responsible for a shooting that left my uncle blind and my cousin having to relearn to walk. My cousin was shot four times. My uncle is blind today because he was shot in the face. Now I won't sit here and even pretend like my uncle and cousin are saints because they are individuals who themselves have commited and participated in homicides in my city. My family has told me the shooting was revenge. It saddens me because my uncle can no longer see.

It's such a scary environment and lifestyle that I come from. I ask myself, how is it that in my city, in my neighborhood, we grow up together knowing each other's entire families, considering each other family, but then somehow get to a point of robbing, killing, and attempting to kill one another? I could of been in the car with my uncle and cousin on the day they got shot. I could of been the third one wounded but didn't make it. God has truly saved me from not only the streets but from myself.

After the shooting, I spoke with both my cousin and uncle over the phone. My cousin is my favorite male cousin. He was like a father to me. Growing up he taught me how to shoot dice, how to sell drugs, how to cook crack, how to hold and shoot guns, how to talk to girls. Almost everything I learnt from the streets, I learnt from him. He is legitimately the biggest thug I know, and I know many. Growing up under him, I seen things I shouldn't have seen. However, in those times, I glorified the streets, but the phone call between us was all fun and games until he started to pick up on how much I had changed. My cousin started to cry saying he did not want to live all his life like he has been. He spoke about how he felt trapped in the streets, said he out there at war by himself, said he wishes I was out. I believe what happened was in that instant, I broke his heart. I created a disconnection that we never had. It brought him to a realization and to tears that me, as his favorite little cousin, the little cousin he practically raised, no longer glorified or admired the streets. It was one of the biggest blessings, but it also now disconnects me from those I love. The reality is I have to leave many behind in order to better myself, and that hurts, but Bailey, there is so much chaos and confusion that has unfolded since and before my incarceration. It's scary and it's unfair to me cause I been changing, and the streets are holding me to this standard expecting me to come home and get in the middle of beef that has nothing to do with me.

Although my uncle has done plenty of dirt, he did not have anything to do with the reason that him and my cousin got shot. The shooters were after my cousin, and I know the streets well. There is a lot of pressure.

Unfair pressure at that. I'm looked at like, look what they did to your uncle. What you gonna do about it? And I want to be successful not vengeful, but how do you communicate that to ones who can't fathom success for themselves?

I also lost a good friend of mine. They say he killed himself, but the police are probably responsible for his death. He never shared suicidal thoughts. The police wanted to question him for murder. He barricaded himself in a bathroom, and now he dead. My family say he had made a Facebook post about killing himself before he goes to jail but it's so hard to accept as true. His family are filing suit alleging the police shot and killed him. I don't know what to believe, and Bailey, it all just put me in a bad state of mind. As strong as I thought I was, I broke, and I wanted to end my own life, so I used a razor blade and just went to town. I ended up in an outside hospital with 15 lacerations. I lost a lot of blood, and although I'm still in prison, this prison is designed to help the mentally ill.

How do you tell someone who feels stuck in the streets that you won't be returning to those very streets that they feel stuck in? My neighbor, he has done 16 years already and has 38 more years to do. How can I look at him and say I'm ready to go home? He is already in his late 40s, early 50s. He will never come home.

Now, the conversation with my uncle went left quick. I can't really explain everything said, but to put it simply, my uncle looks at me like I'm a coward. He doesn't know I been changing over the years, but he and many others are assuming that the events that occured are the reason that I no longer love the streets. People from my past have no idea who I am today, and it hurts a little that they don't understand. Bailey, my friend, I'm not coming back to jail for no one. Period.

I'm doing much better today, but I was very troubled a while back. I'm back on track, and Bailey,

I'm not going back to that lifestyle. In this moment, I'm honestly envisioning me starting my new life in Oregon. I'm so determined to be a person better than whoever this person is. I once thought I was better than this person the streets want me to be, and listen, Bailey, I am so grateful to God that you are here for me and want the best things for me. I don't take you for granted. I hope you all are well. I almost cried reading you say that you care and have thought of me often. I can't stress enough how important it is for us to remain friends through these years. I feel like a big part of my livelihood depends on the people I consider friends and family, so with all of that being said, I need you, Bailey. I don't know a woman like you. You are one of my biggest blessings, and don't take this the wrong way, but I often think of you as my way out the streets. Although I have long ago decided I'm done, I still feel like you are in some way saving me. You're my angel. You're my reminder of how great we all can be. Oh, and I began writing a book. Although I have no experience, I do have a sure vision for it. It will be a self-help book. Until next time, peace and love, my friend.

Sincerely,
Quintavius

GOOD, BETTER, BEST

Bailey

Thank you for the support, I really appreciate it. It's hard to meet wonderful people like you while I'm in the situation I'm in. I'm glad you wrote me and thankful for an opportunity to build up something with you. It feels like we were destined to have contact with each other.

Yes, I want all the luxuries. I didn't come from a wealthy family. I was just a little bit above poverty, so I have that motivational force to want to succeed and be wealthy and be comfortable. And put my family in a better situation, you know? That's why I'm trying to become more knowledgeable and expand my mind. I actually just got done taking an NCRC test. It's sort of like an ACT test. I'm waiting for the results, but I know I did well.

I want to help kids who are in a bad situation. That when they grow up all they would've been is drug dealers and robbers and turn them into lawyers, entrepreneurs, or any career they want to pursue.

My favorite quote is, "Good, better, best, never let it rest, until your good is better, and your better is best." Thanks for supporting me.

Sincerely,
Deion Robinson

I WANT TO BECOME BETTER

Bailey

Hello to you again!

Well, look, I have a lot of dreams that may come true one of these days as long as I keep pushing. Bailey, my dreams are to be big in my music one day, if it's God's will. And my goals are to be there for my kids and watch them grow up to become something in life. Maybe a doctor or a lawyer or something—anything but seeing them come to a prison like me. You ask me who are you and who do you want to become? I want to become someone better than my old self, somebody that everyone looks up to in life. A leader. Bailey, I lay carpet and do roofing for a living. And far as books, I read a lot, really anything that gives me wisdom and knowledge and understanding. Anything that's going to help me change my life and become a better person, I read them. Bailey, you know for many years I didn't know who I was and what I wanted to become in life until God opened my eyes and took away the one thing I loved in my life, and that's my freedom, my kids, and my family. But little by little, God is starting to give me everything back. When I started opening my eyes to reality. And if you ask me, I am thankful for everything God gave me and for your coming into my life as a friend and a penpal during a hard time, so thank you . . .

Love and respect,
Michael Joseph Morris

MY MAIN GOAL

Hey.

I got my results back and scored gold on my NCRC test, so I'm proud of myself for that! Thank you for your support. It will help me get good jobs once I'm released, but my main goal is to have my own businesses and be my own boss. But I know I will have to start somewhere. I actually have been thinking about getting into apprenticeships and trades right when I get out to make a good amount of money.

Well, I'm happy you wrote me. You are someone I needed in my life at the right time to motivate me to become an overachiever. So thank you, Bailey. You play an important role in my life, especially while I'm in prison.

OK so with appearances, would it be okay to have like gold teeth or long hair? I actually like dressing professional. I like wearing suits and polo shirts, so that will be easy for me to adjust to that.

The new location I'm in is way better. I get to be out all day until 12am. And it's less strict than the place I was in. My case manager is supposed to run me down to minimum points and send me to a minimum facility. I'd be able to actually work a job outside of prison for my last year or two. That will be wonderful. I am pretty far from family being here, so that's the only downfall. But I have to make sacrifices to get to where I'm going!

Thank you for keeping in contact with me. It means a lot Bailey! And you wrote me back quicker than usual, so that's amazing lol. Take care Bailey, speak to you soon!

Sincerely,
Deion Robinson

PASSIVE INCOME

Dear Bailey,

I hope this letter finds you enjoying a life full of peace and prosperity in all aspects of your life. I'm glad that you find my life story interesting. I understand that that part of my life made me what I am today but if the truth be told, I would change a lot of my past if I could. I have a lot of good memories but I made a lot of bad decisions.

You asked about my family. I have four older brothers and a little sister. We used to argue a lot, but my sister and I were the babies of the family so we got along good. In fact, here's a short story that kind of shows you how she felt about me. When I was about 8 or 9, we told our dad that we were going to walk down to our grandpa's and go fishing. The first thing our dad told us was to stay out of the boat. Being young and dumb, the first thing we do is get into the boat. She got in front. As I pushed the boat off shore and tried to step into it, the boat started rocking. My sister had never been on a boat so she panicked and tried to stand up. Needless to say the boat capsized with her in the water and me on shore. She started screaming and splashing around yelling that she was drowning, so I jumped in to save her. The thing is I had not learned to swim yet. Anyways, I jump in and realize that the water only comes up to about my chest. I look at my sister and she's still splashing around yelling for me to save her and so on. So I tell her to stand up. I guess that her mind could not process what I was telling her, so I reached over, pulled her up and helped her to shore. To this day, she will tell you that I saved her life. I think that it hurt her more than anyone when I came to prison. Even after all this time that I have been locked up, whenever she comes to see me, she always leaves crying.

My mother and father are another story. My mother worked at our school for almost 30 years. My dad is a preacher. Now that I sit back and think about it, I feel like they understood me more or better than I thought. They always pushed me, but they allowed me to be me. Then again, maybe they didn't understand me either. Everyone else in the family, they make their money work for them. Once a person becomes the master of their money, a whole other life opens up. I hope that you do not think such is just the talk of someone who has been locked up a long time and has not had to face life problems. (Even though that is true!) When I gain my freedom, I plan on developing passive income. Not because I am afraid of hard work, but rather because I now know what to work toward, and I know how to turn my plans into reality.

Bailey, can you imagine how different the world would be if we understood more about how we have power over our life. Most youth are not exposed to bigger dreams and are made to believe that life has a limited number of options.

About my book. It is my desire to try and have it sent to a self-publishing company by the end of the year. Are you still planning on going forward with your book? Youth empowerment is an alarm that needs to be sounded. I know that your time is valuable, and I thank you for allowing me to exchange my thoughts and ideas with you. Keep enjoying life. Be well, my friend!

DeWayne Browning

BOOKS

Dear Bailey,

Hope this letter finds you doing GREAT and that you are happy, safe, and stress-free. I am doing OUTSTANDING right now. I am currently working on two more books with possibly a third one on the horizon. I am trying to get my name (well, pen name) out there so that when my second book comes along, I already have a fan-base built up.

That's great that you're cool with being the main character in my book. It will probably take me about 6-9 months to write the book and get it revised/edited, but I hope that you will be my first reader.

You asked me why I have a pen-name. Well, there are a few reasons. The first being that Stephen King used a pen-name at first. He wrote under the name Richard Bachman and eventually ended up killing off Richard Bachman in one of his books. But not only that, the second reason I chose to write and publish under a pen-name is because I was intrigued with the idea of anonymity like the performer Sia when she first hit stardom. Plus, if the book flopped, it wouldn't be linked to my real name unless I wanted it to be. Many reasons, same motive! Thanks for the compliment about my real name. I find it okay. McManus is way cooler.

I couldn't imagine you ever being a semi-unhappy grump. Your letters just come off with such positivity and grace. So, let your inner beauty shine. Like you, I am very blessed as well. I am grateful, but I would have to multiply that word by a thousand (at least) to give you an accurate description of how I feel.

Take care of yourself, Miss Bailey. Be strong, stay safe. Merry Christmas and Happy New Years!

Sincerely,
John Wilsford

A GOOD AND HONEST LIFE

Hey Bailey,

Got your letter last week and was happy to hear from you. I turned 22 on July 9th, and that was my 4th b-day I've had in prison. It sucks, but I can only blame myself for the situation I'm in and use this time to better myself before I get released. And I do the best I can do each and every day regardless if it's a good or bad day.

My goals as of right now are to try my best to get an A.A. college degree through mail correspondence classes before I get out of prison. Once out, I hope to just live a good and honest life and prove your mistakes do not define who you are. I would also like to speak to troubled youth about their problems with the hope that they can see I've been in the same situations they're in, and I ended up 7 years in prison living like that to try and get them to change their life around.

I hate negativity. It's hard to do good with so much negativity surrounding you. I hate violence when it's unnecessary and too many lives are lost due to gangs. More than anything I hate drugs and myself when I'm on them. I'm a completely different person when I'm on drugs.

I struggle with my drug problem. I have gotten a lot better at it but used to be real weak at caving in to the temptation I had to party and get high. I'm a 22-year-old prisoner with a troubled past who got himself in the situation he's in now through excessive partying and drug use along with illegal activity because he couldn't cope with losing his father so young and fast and cared less about anything he did from there on. I'm an example of the expression, "Don't judge a book by its cover." Regardless, I'm honestly a good and caring person. I would do anything for the ones I love even if it meant going without for myself. I have a big heart and personality with a determination to be successful in life no matter the struggle it takes to finally get there. I am Kelly Evans.

Hope to hear back from you soon. Take care and be safe!

Kelly Evans

WHAT PAIN BRINGS

Inside looking out all he sees is the surface,
It seems like he collected but really nervous,
Diggin' down deep to find his purpose,
Walkin the road torn jeans going shirtless,
He's told he deserves this—a loser, absolutely worthless,
Amounting to curses layin' lines using cursive,
Spittin' verses to escape the cuts he need nurses,
Adrenaline rushin' monster will resurface.
He lurches in shadows and doorways to not be seen,
What he perceive to be white is really green,
He try to comprehend but don't understand a thing,
He need a change of pace need to paint a new scene,
So tell me what this mean when he living a dream,
Realms of darkness all it seem he a suicide king,
Searchin' for his queen she fly away with her wings,
Cool and calm . . . na, this is what his pain brings . . .

By Carlos Lopez-Mata

SMILES THAT I'M HOME

Hello Bailey,

Thank you for your letter. It is always helpful mentally and emotionally to receive letters from people who care about us lesser people here in prison. Thank you also for inquiring about the military for me. It is more of a pipe dream if anything. I screwed up the Marine Corps deal I had in 2015, and in retrospect, traded it for a one-way trip to prison.

Whether joining the Marines at 18 years old would have worked out or not, I do know one thing: coming to prison has been a life changing experience. An eye-opener, let's say.

Although it is stressful being forced into a society behind bars, it is also a blessing in disguise so to speak. How? Well, I'm stuck here in this prison, cut off from both positive and negative stress from the outside world, so no work, no bills, no kids, etc. But I'm stuck with myself in here. I'm 22 years old now. My long, dragged-out point is that I've taken advantage of my time to work on myself. I've come to a maturity level that I fear, had I been on the streets, would not have matured as fast. I'm nowhere near where I can and should be, and I still have faults but can only continue to work on myself no matter what obstacles lay ahead of me.

As for my future plans, my time here in prison is growing short. Six and a half months left in this purgatory. To be honest, I have many hopes and dreams that I hope will come true, but I'm anxious. Upon my release date, I'll be a month shy of being 23 years young with no car, no job, no home, and no money. It'll be as if I'm starting over, and I will be, completely.

I do want a family one day with a beautiful wife and beautiful children in a beautiful house with a nice front and back yard. I long for the day I can get up, go to work, come home to my kids with smiles on their faces that I'm home, to my wife who went out of her way to make dinner for us to eat as a family. Right now, they are dreams and fantasies, and I simply can't wait for it.

Until next time.

Your prison friend,
Timothy Davis

PROVIDE

Bailey,

Hey, what's up! I'm glad to hear back from you. I know that being out there in that world is something else. You have so many things that you want to take care of. I have two beautiful little girls already, so now when I come home, I am financially stable and know that my future is filled with good credit, and I can take on that responsibility to provide for my kids. I want to give my children a childhood that they can always look back to and make them happy. I would not want my kids to go through or grow up the way that I did. You know? I feel that I went through hell and so much pain growing up as a kid just so that my kids won't have to go through anything like that.

My determination to come home and do great things in life is just unbelievable. I look at all the negative things that happened to me from a positive point of view, and it expands my higher thinking and knowledge of life.

How are we going to benefit from communicating with each other? Because I also want to go out there and empower children. I want to turn all this negativity that I have went through in my life and use it in a positive way. I would like for you to help me do that. And yeah, you're right. I don't look at my incarceration as a failure. I just take it as a lesson learned and keep on pushing. I have learned so many great things from this. I'm hoping to be home sometime next year.

Much love and respect to you and your family.
Until next time, take care!

Jorge Orozco

THE ONE THING WE ALL HAVE IN COMMON

Bailey,

Today I got your letter. It honestly made my day. I got the book you sent a few weeks ago, and it's really good. I'm at the part where he talks about transformational vocabulary.

As far as obstacles, it's getting my GED. I have been in prison for 5 years and haven't had one opportunity to get in school. I spoke to the warden, which is a rarity, but it got me nowhere. They say that due to my outdate, every time someone with less time than myself puts in for school, that drops my name on the waitlist. They pretend to not make men with longer sentences a priority, but it's tricky cause there are guys with just as much if not more time than me, but somehow they are in school for five years. I been on this "waitlist," and that's frustrating cause I know that getting my GED will give my future some balance. But I know once I get my shot, I won't look back, but enough of the jailhouse unfairness.

I mentioned old friends not being here for me. The blessing about that is that sometimes friendships just run their course. People will come in our life one season and be gone the next. In all honesty, the friends I lost due to my incarceration aren't true friends anyway. Growing apart from them is one of the best things that could ever happen to me. I'm not that same teen. I'm not interested in the things that once excited me. My old friends are all from the streets. Unfortunately they are not getting the alone time that I am. This time I have utilized to better myself and my future. I'm from the streets, so I know firsthand how it is, but my blessing is being here. I could of been dead. I been shot twice, only 17 years old at the time. I seen a lot and done a lot, but I'm here to talk about it and most importantly learn from it all. I feel saved from that lifestyle and even saved from myself in a sense.

In the future I'm really excited to meet new people and make new friends, really genuine people with compassion, dreams, ambitions, open minds, open hearts. I have no doubt that my future will be one of my biggest blessings. My life is forever changed, and that's for the better. It's all divine intervention. I really changed. I think more clear, and I truly love who I am becoming, and I know my family and new friends will appreciate me, understand me, and never turn their back. I did so much for people who turned their backs on me, but it was me. I invested a lot of time, love, loyalty, money into the wrong people. I know people who only know people like themselves. I know families without dreams, but the one thing we all have in common is that we all want to be loved, understood, and accepted. That's all I want. I'm not going back to a life of becoming blind or getting blindsided. I'm excited to be a true friend of yours. Be safe, take care of yourself, respect yourself. Peace and love.

Sincerely,
Quintavius

LOSING MY VIRGINITY

Hello Bailey,

What's up, Bailey? I hope all is still going well with you over there in Oregon! As far as what it will be like for me upon my release, I believe God will be providing me with a place to live. I'm shooting for a place called Liberty Ministries, a faith-based organization. As for the details of transportation, I dunno yet. It'll be all new for me, but I'll keep you posted.

I am molded into the man I'm meant to be in God's eyes. I've had a change of heart. I desire to do none of the evil I had planned for years. I want good for me and for those I can help in the process.

I always keep in mind, "no matter how bad I think I've got it, someone's got it worse." I really can't wait for these walls here to be no more a part of my life. I wish to excel and for you to be there ("Facebook") to witness and share in delight with my dearest friends and family, because you are a true friend, for you did not forsake me in my situation, you wanted to get to know who I am and not who I was. You are one of a few in the world who truly does not judge a book by its cover. For that your inward beauty outshines the outer beauty.

I will keep you posted! Keep me in your prayers, wish me luck, and hope the best for me.

When I get out, I have a date, a date with the one to whom I'm going to lose my virginity . . . IHOP! I have yet to go there. I'm a fatty for breakfast!

Love, your friend,
Timothy Davis

LOSING MY VIRGINITY: PART 2

Hi Bailey,

It definitely has been a while, and a lot has happened since my release. I was determined to change my life around for the best. Long story short, I went to a homeless shelter due to nowhere to go. I worked and worked all the while saving my money. I then met a woman and began to fall in love with her. Her and I made the sacrifice of sucking up the shitty conditions in order to save. We decided upon having a baby. We then settled upon a 3br house which we now reside in. We also both have our own vehicles. This year our daughter was brought into this world. So that pretty much sums up my last year of freedom.

*   I work for a huge roofing company. I help manage the warehouse and run sales to customers there as well. I also am a key component of ensuring the teams going to the sites have the proper roofing supplies. My probation officer got all mushy because he said I'm his success case. Sometimes I lose sight in prison, so it's nice to hear once in a while that I'm appreciated and seen.*

*   Timothy Davis*

FACTS ABOUT AFTER PRISON

A study by Emory University found that:

- ❖ Individuals who complete some high school courses have recidivism rates around 55%.
- ❖ Vocational training cut recidivism to approximately 30 percent.
- ❖ An associate degree drops the rate to 13.7 percent.
- ❖ A bachelor's degree reduces it to 5.6 percent.
- ❖ A master's brings recidivism to 0 percent.[5]

"If someone in prison receives the opportunity to learn an industrial skill or acquire knowledge in a specialized field, not only do they rarely return to prison (less than 10%), but they also go on to build businesses, create jobs, and inspire their local communities." StandTogether.org[6]

FRIEND NOT FOE

There is a singularity we assign to people we have stigmatized. People in prison are supposed to be scary, mean, dangerous. That has not been my experience. Often, they are people who were born with a disadvantage toward incarceration, such as being born Black, poor, or in an abusive home. None of my pen pals has ever threatened me, scared me, or even been mean to me. Everyone I have ever written has been nothing but kind, grateful, and generous. I have received books, gifts, thank you notes, Mother's Day cards, Christmas cards, even Easter cards, stunning artwork, and the kindest, most thoughtful letters. In the following letters, I hope you see that people are just people no matter their circumstances. They are undeserving of any stigmatization. These friends of mine could never be reduced to a singular identity.

Rosaria Butterfield writes in her book, *The Gospel Comes with a House Key,* "Radically ordinary hospitality—those who live it see strangers as neighbors and neighbors as family of God. They recoil at reducing a person to a category or a label. They see God's image reflected in the eyes of every human being on earth." When I read the following letters, it became impossible for me to reduce my friends to any label. God's image is so obviously reflected in every man who got sent to prison and took the time to write me a letter.

BIG MO

Bailey

I've had a somewhat major shake up in my routine here on the unit. I really can't go into it now, but things got real crazy for me about a week ago. I'm still waiting for everything to shake out.

So often there are not enough volunteers to fill the five or six functions that arise Monday, Wednesday, and Thursday evenings we have meetings. So I've given the group leaders permission to insert my name into any of the unfilled roles that need to be filled. And at work I've become more proactive. That's a very "work-intensive" step, but that's the purpose of it. So I'm taking these steps, developing a routine, making myself available, and I feel putting my thoughts on paper. All of these are designed with the purpose of getting me out of my head and into reality. To put my ideas that I've spent so much time on before people that can benefit from them. People who can give me feedback on them. For so long I've been very introverted and anti-social because of self-esteem issues. It took many, many years until I realized that isolation is the worst thing for me. Every time I've isolated myself, everytime that I've disconnected from my environment, every single time, it was the beginning of my undoing.

I believe that I have within me the ingredients for a successful life. But I don't have the habits to match. I remember 20+ years ago, my brother told me about a book that changed his life at the time. It was Stephen Covey's, 7 Habits of Highly Effective People. I had heard about that book for years at that time and had read some reviews about the book but had never read it. But for the last five years or so, this book has been popping up in conversations, books, etc. as if it's time for me to read it. And after reading Darren Hardy's book,

Covey's book would dovetail smoothly. It's in our library so I'll order it. It's about time to get this life rolling. Get "Big Mo" on my side. I want to thank you, Bailey, for this book. I will keep it because I'm afraid someone will just throw it into their locker, and no one else will be able to benefit from its wisdom, so I will pass it around, planting the seed and hoping it will awaken others to their hidden/suppressed potential.

Okay, Bailey. I haven't learned all that I'll learn from Darren Hardy nor all that I'll learn from you. Till next time.

Your friend Floyd

I WANT TO BE SPECIAL TO SOMEBODY

Dear Bailey,

I have so much more I'd like you to know about myself. I take businesses, my career very seriously. I try to take my future seriously, but every time I try to involve someone in my life, I get hurt. I'm a very good man, but I just can't find a girl I can trust or depend on. I've learned to depend on nobody but myself. I get no financial help in here at all, but I live better than people whose families send them a hundred dollars a week. I don't do anything illegal to live good in here. I'm a business man. I am very self disciplined to survive. If I had a family, I could provide for them from in here. I actually pay child support.

I have a lot of leadership qualities, which is why I love to help and teach people things. On the streets, I would donate bouncy castles to the kids at the boys and girls club three times a year. I would deliver food to families on Thanksgiving every year. I would also deliver toys to children with Toys for Tots for Christmas. Do you believe in God? Do you ever go to church? I've lived a rough life, Bailey. I've done things that were wrong. But I've done more good than I have bad. And I feel that God will bless me in amazing ways and finally bring that special someone into my life after these obstacles I'm going through now.

I really want to be special to somebody. I deserve happiness. Are you happy? I truly hope you are. One thing I know we have in common is we both have big hearts and like helping others. But for me, it always bites me in the butt. I've been wondering what it would be like to travel and move from state to state every few years. What do you want for yourself? Do you have plans? I have big plans for my future, but I have to finish paying for the mistakes I've made. Twenty three months left out of eighty four.

Are you in a relationship? Have you ever been married? I've been proposed to three times, and I've turned all three down. I've never been married. I didn't turn them down because I don't want to get married. I just believe it takes more than six months to make that kind of commitment. I believe that marriage is finding a person you can love for the rest of their life, a person that has your back no matter what. You have to support one another and make certain sacrifices for each other. I think communication is one of the most important things. I feel I have to be compassionate towards her feelings. The most important thing is to tell her you love her as many times as you can everyday, so there is no doubt in her mind. Those are rules I set for myself. To provide and protect. Looking forward to the next day with her everyday. That to me is a dream I'd love to live.

I was raised to always do things right the first time and you will never have to go back and fix it again. I wish I could have lived my life by that rule. It just goes to show I'm far from perfect. The last letter I wrote will probably take months to get to you because it's under investigation from the last yard for something I had nothing to do with. Just being a person with a good reputation can get you in trouble. My prayers and best wishes go out to you every morning and every night. I have lots of letters to mail out to you.

Yours truly,
Jason Moore

MATCH.COM

Bailey,

The game of questions.
   Well here's your answers:
   I listen to music for fun. It keeps my mind free.
   I used to do drugs. Cocke-cane, to be exact.
   I do not smoke.
   I do have many regrets in life.
   There was a teacher that impacted my life when I was younger. Once, she bought me some shoes when I didn't have any good ones. I believe it played a big part in me being so giving to others. I will give my last to someone I don't know if they ask.
   The person in my life I'm closest with is my mom. She's everything to me.
   I most desire a big family, loving wife, and big Christmases and family reunions.
   My favorite movie is The Notebook. *I watch it everytime it comes on. My first love introduced me to it, and I never let it go.*
   I haven't made it far enough in meditation to know my spiritual animal.
   It's crazy the path I took because I've always wanted to help people. I wanted to be a police officer or a choreographer.
   If I could own any business, it would be match. com. Creating love seems the best to suit me.
   If I wrote a book, it would be a romance novel called Time. *(Coming soon . . .)*
   I feel a lot of emotions a day, too many to keep track of.

                              Respectfully,
                              KeShawn Jones

A LITTLE MOTIVATION THING I WROTE

"Why do people settle for less when they are worth more?"

It's easy to get stuck and stagnate in a situation where we have no knowledge of ourselves or a way of betterment. The old saying goes, "If you knew better, you'd do better." As people, we care to know the truth about our situation and still accept it because it meets the needs of the moment. We get caught up in the moment, and in doing so, we sacrifice our morals, happiness, and true identities. Instead of loving ourselves more and being patient, we rush for that microwave gratification. A quick fix that works right then but in the long run drains us physically, emotionally, and spiritually because we don't know our worth.

When you're mindful of who you are and what your net worth is, you create a standard that you would not go beneath. You demand more because you're worth it. You're not going to trade a hundred dollar bill for pennies? You're not going to trade gold for copper? So why trade yourself for anything that is not of equal value or more? Just another jewel to ponder on. You polish it the way you want it to shine.

Gunner White

SOME OF MY PASSIONS

Bailey,

Hello! I pray that this letter reaches you in the greatest spirits, health, and I hope all is well. It's cool to see that you understand my state of being able to change, although instability wasn't something easy for me. I struggle everyday to get where I want and need to be. Rehabilitating myself is a process that at times is stressful but worthwhile. Being that I had to find true purpose in life on my own. I had to regain autonomy over my destiny so I can find what some of my defects are that hinder me. In the past, I would get praised for my ignorance, and it took a while to notice that everything I got praised for was the BS that was in the way. Now I'm just healing and repairing my life while trying to decode this matrix called life so I can succeed internally and externally.

Like you, I want to help people as well, although I want to take a different approach. One of my goals is to be a film writer and producer. Watching the show Blackish and understanding the content of each episode, I see that they all serve a purpose besides entertaining, and are enlightening America on the everyday struggles of African Americans.

Some of my passions are cooking, being the best father I can, and helping people. Also, I have a passion for healthy living. Something I know now that I wish I would have known is how important education is, the importance of parenting, and the effects of being in a gang. The advice that I have for kids who are struggling would be to know that you too can be in horrible situations like others. Through hard work and dedication you can obtain anything you want. Understand that your self-worth is priceless, and if nobody sees that then they don't want to see you make it.

No matter your circumstances, you can always be bigger and greater. You must manifest your own destiny. What you put out is what you will get back. Thoroughly think things through because impulsivity will lead to regrets. Understand others before you judge. When you encounter positive influences, trust their process and create a paradigm that fits your life.

Don Real

PERCEPTION

Bailey,

Hey, hey, hey! It always puts a smile on my face when I get a letter from you. I don't believe I've ever thanked you for not judging me because I'm a "prisoner." We people on the inside tend to have a negative stigma attached to us, so people judge . . . but not you. No, you're not everybody else. You're you. You're Bailey. So thank you for ensuring the peace and happiness behind the smile I carry. Since I leave June 13th, I expect this will be my last letter to you in prison, so I'm going to say, hold onto this letter.

As for the article you sent me, very inspiring. On a related topic, when we look to other men and women as our idols or heroes, it creates a dependence on replicating their lives to find what everybody wants: happiness. When one of these heroes falls, we are destroyed. So the topic of happiness in the article says, "Let go of the idea of happiness you had in your mind, and instead, [start] being grateful for what you already have." I have personally learned to be content with my belongings, my surroundings, my friends and family, and in doing so, left off my shoulders a weight no one should carry—feeling inadequate.

This article sparked a thought. The way you look at things, perception, is powerful. To one man, 1 and 1 might be 2, but to another, it might be 11. We choose to see the negative in situations or the positives, and that is important to remember.

I hope this letter can fill you with peace and glue a smile to your face.

Lots of love back to you friend,
Timothy Davis

LET ME ASK A QUESTION

Bailey,

Thank you for such an unexpected letter. I guess first impressions are very long-lasting ones? I just got out of the hole December 15th. Me and my lil brother did a 120. Sometimes the only way to think of a new game plan is a timeout. So tell me, how is your brother and the kids you're taking care of? Lately I've been pondering life from a very philosophical standpoint. Philo in Greek means love. Sophical means wisdom. The wisdom in life is that the clock is always counting down, counting down till we cease to breathe. Let me ask you a serious question: Are you trying to find yourself or create yourself? What do you think your role and contribution is in society? No one's role is less important than another person's. Hopefully this letter reaches you in good time and good health.

Damien Lanson

ONE FLAW IN WOMEN

Women are a special creation by God, and you are a perfect example. You have a kiss that can cure anything from a scraped knee to a broken heart, and she will do everything with only two hands. She heals herself when she's sick and can work 18-hour days. She is tough and can endure and accomplish anything she sets her mind to. Women are truly amazing. She has high, unreachable love strengths that amaze men. They are capable of carrying heavy burdens, but they hold happiness, love and joy. They smile when they want to scream. They sing when they want to cry. They cry when they are happy. They fight for what they believe in and stand up to injustice. They do not take "NO" for an answer when they feel there is a better solution. They love unconditionally. They are happy when they hear about a birth or a wedding, and their heart breaks when a loved one dies. They grieve at the loss of a family member. Yet, they are strong when they think no strength is left. They know a hug and kiss can heal a broken heart. They will drive, fly, walk, run, or e-mail you to show you how much they care. The heart of a woman is what makes the world keep turning. They bring joy, hope, and love, have compassion, and give moral support to their family and friends.

Women have vital things to say and everything to give. However, if there is one flaw in women, it's that they truly forget what they are truly worth...

Please, do not forget what you are truly worth...

Wyatt Hernandez

THINGS YOU WOULD PROBABLY PUT PAST ME

Bailey...

I didn't think I was ever going to hear from you again. I moved prisons, so it took the prison I moved from a long time to forward your letter and picture to me. I was happy to see you didn't forget about me.

I am into a lot of things you would probably put past me. Like I am into philosophy. I like to read nothing but personal development books and financial development books. I like Robert Kyosaki and Napoleon Hill. Rich Dad Poor Dad is my favorite book. I want to read some Tony Robbins books, but they don't have any of his books in the library here. My uncle was supposed to send me some books. I am still waiting. If you want, you can send me some books.

What kind of book are you writing? How old are your kids? Do you really like rap music?

Kalan Sturdy

I HEARD A STORY

Bailey

I heard a story about a woman who was really quite remarkable and thought I would share it with you. This lady met a man that she fell in love with. One of the things she loved about him was his smell, which she described as a "male musk." If I remember correctly they married, and about 10 to 15 years later he got a different job. After a while, she said his smell changed. She described this new smell as kind of "yeasty," and not pleasant at all. The lady endured it for a while thinking it related to his new job. Eventually, she suggested he take longer baths to rid himself of the smell. He grew very irritated about her complaint. One night she woke up, and her husband was assaulting her while making weird noises. She suggested that he go to the hospital. Long story short, they found out he had Parkinson's Disease. The couple signed up for a support group, and the first time they went, the wife was overwhelmed by that "yeasty" smell throughout the room. As they were introduced to different people, she realized that the smell was coming from THE PEOPLE! Some more pronounced than others, but all had the smell! She mentioned this to her husband's doctor, and he wrote her off as kinda looney. But then he heard how dogs could smell cancer and also smell seizures before they happened. So he (the doctor) decided to do a test; he sent out t-shirts to Parkinson's patients to wear for a weekend but not wash as well as folks who did not have the disease. He then collected the shirts (randomly numbered) and sent them to the woman. She correctly identified all the shirts that had been worn by Parkinson's sufferers! One shirt she picked was a man's who had not been diagnosed, but a few months later THAT MAN TOO HAD BEEN DIAGNOSED!!! Come to find out the woman's nose is so sensitive, she can detect cancer and a couple of other diseases. Her husband has since passed away, but before he did, he told her to keep doing the work and to not give up because of all the people she could help. Isn't that awesome, Bailey? Stay safe, my friend. Stay prayerful. And may God bless all that you put your hands to.

*Your friend,
Floyd*

TUMBLING

Dear Ms. McManus

Hello my name is Kadeem Duke. I'm 26. One of your letters fell into my lap because one of your teens needed help comprehending your questions and request. Well, let me tell you a little bit about me. I'm from the south side of Chicago but always had good surroundings, becoming a member of a famous tumbling team at 12 years old. From that time til 2011, I've traveled the world performing at Chicago Bulls games, block-club parties, high schools, colleges, parades . . . any place you name, I've been there. During that time, I picked up the talent of blogging and creating videos to post on social media. My videos range from dancing to gymnastics. From daily vlogs all the way to RIP tributes for teens who have gotten killed in some of the toughest neighborhoods in Chicago. My current incarceration does not reflect the man I was or the man I am today. I would love to work on future projects with you. I pray I can become some type of assistant to your project.

Take care. Sincerely,
Kadeem Duke

PLAN A AND PLAN B

Dear Bailey,

Please allow me to introduce myself. My name is Albert B. Holly. I have been a writer since I was in the sixth grade. My first short was called "The Adventures of Super Ray." It was a comic book about a pickle that saved other pickles from being eaten, used in sandwiches, etc. Super Ray was a green pickle with a purple cape. He met his demise when he reached into a blender to save another pickle. Needless to say, when the blender was turned on, Super Ray and the pickle were cast into spin-cycle, and it was a wrap! No more Super Ray.

Since I've been in prison, I've written 30 novels, 15 screen plays, and a couple of graphic novels as I am an artist as well. I have about 4 and ½ years to go. Then I'll be looking to become a published writer. My 'A-plan' is to drive trucks. My 'B-plan' is writing.

In closing, I'd like to establish a friendship with you if you're open to that! I must tell you, I am an innocent man, wrongfully convicted, but it doesn't much matter at this point. God has blessed me to do the time and master the craft of writing.

Thank you for your time, Bailey! God bless you!

Albert B. Holly

STOP, LOOK, AND LISTEN

Bailey

Did I tell you that I would not mention C_ _ _ D in my letters to you during this "episode" in history? Well, I'll keep my word.

But I will tell you this. I have been restored the status and privileges that I lost last May! (WEE!) I have been moved back to the least restrictive side of this prison. But I was not given a job. I really need to work. But I always look around for the PURPOSE of the situation I find myself in. Too often I've focused on the mechanism (event) that led to the circumstance, and I'm not saying that part isn't important, but I've realized that this part is just as important if not more important.

That event was simply the mechanism that FATE, GOD or whatever used in order to get you where you are in order for you to complete the next phase of your (my) life. There is someone or something here that is critical to my development, progress, etc.

So I've learned to "stop, look, and listen." I think that the most valuable lesson I've learned about my life is that if it were solely up to me, I would have been a total mess physically, mentally, spiritually, and every other way. But looking back over my life, I've been saved or spared from the worst of the consequences of my actions. And situation after situation I've gotten through with minimal damage or nowhere near the punishment I should have gotten. I had to ask myself, WHY? Who or what was looking out for me. But more importantly, why? What is so special about me? Why was I spared? Am I supposed to do something? Is that why I'm being spared? It's these questions that nudged me toward the outlook I have now. I just try to view things as being larger than myself. Kinda like a relay race, the baton has been handed to me. What will I do with it? I may not actually cross the finish line myself. That's not my position. My job is simple: don't drop the baton! Run my leg. Do my job. Don't die with the music still inside me!

That's what I need you for Bailey. To be a sounding board. A friend. An outlet for some of this stuff. Sometimes I'll shut down for a while, but I'm still reading, writing, thinking, and trying to move forward.

Thank you for being that friend, ear, sounding board, and outlet for me, Bailey. Thank you for your time, your responses, your gifts, your encouragements, and all that you've been. Thank you.

Your Friend
Floyd Ike Williams

AFTER THE FACT

Eight years have passed since I wrote my first pen pal. So much has changed in my life and in the lives of people I have written.

Timothy Davis was released from prison, got married, and has a daughter. His parole officer called Timothy his "success story." Timothy did go to treatment for alcohol abuse some time after he was released but is in recovery now and doing well.

Jason Moore got out of prison and, of course, immediately started multiple successful businesses. He has an electrician company, refurbishes and sells cars, details cars, and remodels mobile homes. He purchased his dream truck (a Ford F150), is engaged, and is taking good care of his children. Jason promised his daughter a new car upon her graduation from high school.

Quintavius Emmers is still incarcerated but has a release date set for about six months from now, though release dates often change, and his release date has been moved forward many times. In his letters, he expressed despair over being unable to attend school during his incarceration due to long wait lists and a lack of educational opportunities. He was finally admitted to a general education program where he is working toward his GED. He has also been diligent in writing music and working toward a musical career. He developed a friendship with a producer in the music business that has turned into frequent phone calls with the producer and his wife. The relationship began when Quintavius shipped an expensive cigar to the producer's office, something he knew the producer enjoyed. Quintavius created an album, has been recording songs during phone calls with his mother, and even obtained copyrights to some of his music.

Damien Lanson and I have grown closer over the years. I have even been able to visit him a couple times. Outside the prison he is in, there sits a statue of a barefoot and shirtless man cradling a bird. Green moss lies across his chest. A hawk rests against his leg. His fingers gently touch the top of its head. The bird leans toward him like a child toward a loving parent. The man returns its gaze with tender eyes. The statue overwhelmed me when I saw it on my way into this caged and sterile environment. It is symbolic of the qualities I witness in these men—my pen pals, my friends. Many have this quiet they seem to hold within them, as if not just seeking a way out but a better way. Damien did not complain during our visit. He asked questions. I showed up unannounced, and he treated me like a friend. I am grateful for that friendship.

Flloyd Ike Williams was released as you saw in his letter titled, "My Freedom." The first thing he did when he got out was make a video diving into the story of the prodigal son—a story that has resonated with me. He found work, but it has proven to be below a living wage. Though he was not overweight, Flloyd lost 55 pounds shortly after his release. I worry for him and hope he finds opportunities to coach younger men as he once did in prison. His letters always fascinated me, and I know struggling young men could gain a lot from his wisdom, especially after his experience serving around 30 years in prison.

As for me, life is completely different from when I wrote the first chapter of this book, "How It Started." When I first started writing people in prison, I was dating a woman whom I ended up marrying, took in three foster children, and was raising my teenage brother and my biological son. I do not have any way to explain what I am about to tell you other than trauma, youth, health problems, and confusion. What I experienced in my personal life was an impetus for writing but not the point of this story, so I didn't focus on it. However, it feels important for me to say that I am not gay; I was confused. I wanted to be fulfilled by a relationship with a woman so badly so that I could stay with my wife. I tried because she was and is an incredible person. She is selfless and kind and hard-working and overall one of the sweetest, most giving people I have ever known.

I considered staying with her for the children. In the end, I decided that would not be the kind of example I wanted to set. I would not want them to live inauthentically, especially in what I believe to be the most important area of life—marriage. So we divorced. The relationship became hostile, and it ended up being better for my ex-wife to adopt our foster children without me. It was the hardest choice I have ever made, and I struggled with depression after I made it. I still believe it was the right thing to do. My ex-wife adopted the children on her own and is now in a loving and committed partnership with another woman. I see the kids occasionally, but it is not enough. I miss them, and I wish I was still their mom. It took time and intention, but my biological son and I have been healing. We created a good life, a life we can be proud of. We are together, and we are happy.

Still, as with my pen pals who look for not just a way out, but a better way, I too want to be more loving, more authentic—a better mom, a better writer, someone who gives back and makes an impact on the world, and someday, a wife. I have so much left to do. That is what will have to remain unwritten for now. What comes after the trauma? After the mistakes? After we try and fail and fail again? I pray every day, for my pen pals and for me, that God will rush into our lives and guide the way forward.

I still write to seven people regularly and occasionally hear from other pen pals. Statistically speaking, some of my pen pals have probably returned to prison, but if they have, I have not heard from them. The men I write today have become like old friends. We know so much about each other and, through our communication, have seen each other through joy and hardship. I cherish my friendships with them.

Every letter I ever received is in my hallway closet, stacked and sealed within ziploc bags. Occasionally, I retrieve the letters and flip through them slowly. I am in awe that I was the one to receive these letters. I examine the names, the beautiful drawings, the handwriting, the postage stamps of flags and birds, the little slips of paper inside reminding me that this, indeed, came from a correctional facility. And I am grateful. Grateful to have known these men and grateful to have gotten a chance to know the truth: that people are so much more than the worst mistake they ever made, that the criminal justice system is not just, and that, through changes such as educational opportunities, our nation can drastically reduce recidivism. So many futures are in our hands. My life seemed to refuse to move forward until I shared this truth. These stories stopped me in my tracks and demanded to be told.

Reader, are you listening?

DRAWINGS

My pen pals have been extremely generous. I have received numerous portraits drawn of me, drawings for my children, detailed calligraphy within many of the letters I have received, holiday cards, and intricate, handmade, Native American beaded jewelry. These are some of my most prized possessions. In the following pages, I share a small selection of what I have received.

By Keshawn Jones

By Abraham Johnson

By Benjamin Guzman

Sincerely, Your Friend

By Quintavius Emmers

By Andres Dixon

By Dale Walker

275 | *Sincerely, Your Friend*

By Dominic Sanchez

By Dominic Sanchez

277 | Sincerely, Your Friend

By Donavon Mendez

By Matthew Navarro

> **"Everything But You"**
>
> Everything takes time but you... learning something new takes time... Trusting takes time... Forgiving takes time... Healing takes time... Love takes time... Everything takes time but you... The mail takes time... A prison sentence takes time... Maturity takes time... this poem takes time... Everything takes time but you...
>
> A relationship takes time... A friendship takes time... A companionship takes time... Everything takes time but you... Success takes time... Progress takes time... Everything takes time but you... and my conclusion for believing in such truth is in your letters, your letters not only make my day -- they make you an investor whom has invested into my character.
>
> Everything takes time but you... Bailey, you truly have given me the very thing that everything takes... Time!

By Quintavius Emmers

By Quintavius Emmers

By Jason Moore

By Dominic Sanchez

Left: A photo of me at the fish market where, between customers, I read and responded to most of these letters.

Below: My son at our kitchen table while I respond to letters. I tried to include something for my pen pals to enjoy as you can see with the inspirational quotes and articles in this photo.

NOTES

CHILDHOOD TRAUMA

1. Cohen, A. (2002). Wisdom of the Heart. Hay House, Incorporated.
2. Cantürk, M., Faraji, H., & Tezcan, A. (2021). The relationship between childhood traumas and crime in male prisoners. Anatolian Journal of Psychiatry, 22, 1–5. https://doi.org/10.5455/apd.111825
3. About Us | Amen Clinics. (2022). Amen Clinics. https://www.amenclinics.com/about-us/
4. Winfrey, O. (2022). What Happened to You? Conversations on Trauma, Resilience, and Healing (Main Market ed.). Bluebird.
5. Childhood Trauma Statistics. (2022). Compassion Prison Project. https://compassionprisonproject.org/childhood-trauma-statistics/

JUVENESCENCE

1. Crone, E. A., & Dahl, R. E. (2012). Understanding adolescence as a period of social-affective engagement and goal flexibility. Nature Reviews Neuroscience, 13(9), 636–650. https://doi.org/10.1038/nrn3313
2. Popma, A., Vermeiren, R., Geluk, C. A., Rinne, T., van den Brink, W., Knol, D. L., Jansen, L. M., van Engeland, H., & Doreleijers, T. A. (2007). Cortisol Moderates the Relationship between Testosterone and Aggression in Delinquent Male Adolescents. Biological Psychiatry, 61(3), 405–411. https://doi.org/10.1016/j.biopsych.2006.06.006
3. Peper, J. S., & Dahl, R. E. (2013). The Teenage Brain. Current Directions in Psychological Science, 22(2), 134–139. https://doi.org/10.1177/0963721412473755
4. Ulmer, J. T., & Steffensmeier, D. (2014). The age and crime relationship: Social variation, social explanations. In The Nurture Versus Biosocial Debate in Criminology: On the Origins of Criminal Behavior and Criminality (pp. 377-396). SAGE Publications Inc. https://doi.org/10.4135/9781483349114.n23
5. Ulmer, J. T., & Steffensmeier, D. (2014). The age and crime relationship: Social variation, social explanations. In The Nurture Versus Biosocial Debate in Criminology: On the Origins of Criminal Behavior and Criminality (pp. 377-396). SAGE Publications Inc. https://doi.org/10.4135/9781483349114.n23
6. Popma, A., Vermeiren, R., Geluk, C. A., Rinne, T., van den Brink, W., Knol, D. L., Jansen, L. M., van Engeland, H., & Doreleijers, T. A. (2007). Cortisol Moderates the Relationship between Testosterone and Aggression in Delinquent Male Adolescents. *Biological Psychiatry, 61*(3), 405–411. https://doi.org/10.1016/j.biopsych.2006.06.006

7. Alexander, M. (2020). *The New Jim Crow.* Amsterdam University Press.; National Advisory Commission on Criminal Justice Standards and Goals, Task Force Report on Corrections (Washington, DC: Government Printing Office, 1973), 358.; Ibid., 597.

8. Nonprofit Risk Management Center. (2017, January 12). *Perspectives on Gangs and GangViolence.* https://nonprofitrisk.org/resources/articles/perspectives-on-gangs-and-gang-violence/#:%7E:text=Demographic%20studies%20of%20gangs%20cited,for%20longer%20periods%20of%20time

FATHERLESSNESS

1. "The Extent of Fatherlessness," National Center for Fathering, Fathering in America Poll, 1999, downloaded from http://www.fathers.com/1999research/extent.html on June 12, 1999.

2. Nonprofit Risk Management Center. (2024, September 25). Perspectives on Gangs and Gang Violence | Nonprofit Risk Management Center. https://nonprofitrisk.org/resources/perspectives-on-gangs-and-gang-violence/

3. Aacap. (n.d.). Teen brain: behavior, problem solving, and decision making. https://www.aacap.org/AACAP/Families_and_Youth/Facts_for_Families/FFF-Guide/The-Teen-Brain-Behavior-Problem-Solving-and-Decision-Making-095.aspx

4. McDaniel, D. D. (2012). Risk and protective factors associated with gang affiliation among high-risk youth: a public health approach. Injury Prevention, 18(4), 253–258. https://doi.org/10.1136/injuryprev-2011-040083; HILL, K. G., HOWELL, J. C., HAWKINS, J. D., & BATTIN-PEARSON, S. R. (1999). Childhood Risk Factors for Adolescent Gang Membership: Results from the Seattle Social Development Project. Journal of Research in Crime and Delinquency, 36(3), 300–322. https://doi.org/10.1177/0022427899036003003

5. Agnafors, S., Bladh, M., Svedin, C. G., & Sydsjö, G. (2019). Mental health in young mothers, single mothers and their children. BMC Psychiatry, 19(1). https://doi.org/10.1186/s12888-019-2082-y; What Are The Effects On Children Of Single Parents? (2017, November 17). EverydayHealth.Com. https://www.everydayhealth.com/kids-health/what-are-effects-on-children-single-parents/

6. Facing Facts: Public Attitudes and Fiscal Realities in Five Stressed States. (2010). *The Pew Center on the States.*

7. Brown, D. (2018, June 18). *Fatherlessness is harder on Father's Day, but "father figures," other role models fill in (usatoday.com).* Parenting with PACEs. https://www.pacesconnection.com/g/Parenting-with-ACEs/blog/fatherlessness-is-harder-on-father-s-day-but-father-figures-other-role-models-fill-in-usatoday-com

8. "The Extent of Fatherlessness," National Center for Fathering, Fathering in America Poll, 1999, downloaded from http://www.fathers.com/1999research/extent.html on June 12, 1999.

9. Childhood Trauma Statistics. (2022). Compassion Prison Project. https://compassionprisonproject.org/childhood-trauma-statistics/

10. Facing Facts: Public Attitudes and Fiscal Realities in Five Stressed States. (2010). *The Pew Center on the States.*

DRUGS

1. *Incarceration/HealthyPeople 2020.* (2022). HealthyPeople.Gov. https://www.healthypeople.gov/2020/topics-objectives/topic/social-determinants-health/interventions-resources/incarceration#34
2. One in 31: The Long Reach of American Corrections. (2009). *The Pew Charitable Trusts.*
3. Alexander, M. (2020). *The New Jim Crow.* Amsterdam University Press.
4. Vagins, D. J., & McCurdy, J. (2006). Cracks in the System: Twenty Years of the Unjust Federal Crack Cocaine Law. *American Civil Liberties Union.*; Alexander, M. (2020). *The New Jim Crow.* Amsterdam University Press.
5. Benforado, A. (2016). *Unfair: The New Science of Criminal Injustice* (Reprint ed.). Crown.
6. One in 31: The Long Reach of American Corrections. (2009). *The Pew Charitable Trusts.*
7. Alexander, M. (2020). *The New Jim Crow.* Amsterdam University Press.; Mauer, M. (2010). *Race to Incarcerate.* New York: The New York Press.
8. United States Sentencing Commission. (2017, October). *Mandatory Minimum Penalties for Drug Offenses in the Federal Criminal Justice System.* https://www.ussc.gov/sites/default/files/pdf/research-and-publications/research-publications/2017/20171025_Drug-Mand-Min.pdf

SENTENCING

1. Alexander, M. (2020). *The New Jim Crow.* Amsterdam University Press.
2. *Ibid.*
3. *Ibid.*; Scott Andron, "SWAT: Coming to a Town Near You?" Miami Herald, May 20, 2002.
4. Alexander, M. (2020). *The New Jim Crow.* Amsterdam University Press.
5. *Ibid.*; Skinner v. Railway Labor Executive Association, 489 U.S. 602, 641 (1980), Marshall, J., dissenting.
6. Alexander, M. (2020). *The New Jim Crow.* Amsterdam University Press.; Mauer, M. (2010). *Race to Incarcerate.* New York: The New York Press.
7. Joseph Treaster, "Two Federal Judges, in Protest, Refuse to Accept Drug Cases," New York Times, Apr. 17, 1993.; Alexander, M. (2020). *The New Jim Crow.* Amsterdam University Press.
8. Alexander, M. (2020). *The New Jim Crow.* Amsterdam University Press.; Chris Carmody, "Revolt to Sentencing Is Gaining Momentum," National Law Journal, May 17, 1993, 10.
9. Alexander, M. (2020). *The New Jim Crow.* Amsterdam University Press.

10. *Ibid.* Special to The New York Times, "Criticizing Sentencing Rules, US Judge Resigns," New York Times, Sept. 30, 1990.

11. United States Sentencing Commission. (2017, October). *Mandatory Minimum Penalties for Drug Offenses in the Federal Criminal Justice System.* https://www.ussc.gov/sites/default/files/pdf/research-and-publications/research-publications/2017/20171025_Drug-Mand-Min.pdf

12. *Prison Conditions.* (2021, March 10). Equal Justice Initiative. https://eji.org/issues/prison-conditions/; Bureau of Justice Statistics, "Summary Report: Expenditure and Employment Data for the Criminal Justice System 1978" (Sept 1980).

13. School, S. L. (2022). *Three Strikes Basics.* Stanford Law School. https://law.stanford.edu/three-strikes-project/three-strikes-basics/

14. Taibbi, M. (2013, March 27). *Cruel and Unusual Punishment: While Wall Street crooks walk, thousands sit in California prisons for life over crimes as trivial as stealing socks.* Rolling Stone. https://www.rollingstone.com/politics/politics-news/cruel-and-unusual-punishment-the-shame-of-three-strikes-laws-92042/

15. *Ibid.*

16. School, S. L. (2022). *Three Strikes Basics.* Stanford Law School. https://law.stanford.edu/three-strikes-project/three-strikes-basics/.

17. Alexander, M. (2020). *The New Jim Crow.* Amsterdam University Press.

18. Benforado, A. (2016). *Unfair: The New Science of Criminal Injustice* (Reprint ed.). Crown.

19. Williams, S. C. P. (2014, April 28). *Science.* AAAS. https://www.science.org/content/article/more-4-death-row-inmates-may-be-innocent#:%7E:text=One%20in%2025%20criminal%20defendants,exonerations%20across%20the%20United%20States.

20. Hinton, A. R., Hardin, L. L., & Stevenson, B. (2019). *The Sun Does Shine: How I Found Life, Freedom, and Justice* (Reprint ed.). St. Martin's Griffin.

21. Marc Mauer and Ryan S. King, Schools and Prisons: Fifty Years After Brown v. Board of Education (Washington, DC: Sentencing Project, 2004), 4.; Alexander, M. (2020). *The New Jim Crow.* Amsterdam University Press.

22. Alexander, M. (2020). *The New Jim Crow.* Amsterdam University Press.

23. Laura Parker, "8 Years in a Louisiana Jail but He Never Went to Trial," USA Today, Aug 29, 2005.

24. Williams, S. C. P. (2014, April 28). *Science.* AAAS. https://www.science.org/content/article/more-4-death-row-inmates-may-be-innocent#:%7E:text=One%20in%2025%20criminal%20defendants,exonerations%20across%20the%20United%20States.

25. *Prison Conditions.* (2021, March 10). Equal Justice Initiative. https://eji.org/issues/prison-conditions/; Bureau of Justice Statistics, "Summary Report: Expenditure and Employment Data for the Criminal Justice System 1978" (Sept 1980).

26. School, S. L. (2022). *Three Strikes Basics.* Stanford Law School. https://law.stanford.edu/three-strikes-project/three-strikes-basics/

27. Alexander, M. (2020). *The New Jim Crow.* Amsterdam University Press.

28. Bureau of Justice Statistics. (n.d.). *Lifetime Likelihood of Going to State or Federal Prison.* https://bjs.ojp.gov/content/pub/pdf/Llgsfp.pdf

PRISON LIFE

1. Stevenson, B. (2015). *Just Mercy: A Story of Justice and Redemption* (Reprinted.). One World.
2. *Ibid.*
3. *Ibid.*
4. *Ibid.*
5. *Ibid.*
6. *Ibid.*
7. *Ibid.*
8. *Ibid.*
9. Initiative, P. P. (2020, December 2). *No escape: The trauma of witnessing violence in prison.* Prison Policy Initiative. https://www.prisonpolicy.org/blog/2020/12/02/witnessing-prison-violence/
10. The Urban Institute, Kim, K., Becker-Cohen, M., & Serakos, M. (2015, March). *The Processing and Treatment of Mentally Ill Persons in the Criminal Justice System.* The Urban Institute. https://www.urban.org/sites/default/files/publication/48981/2000173-The-Processing-and-Treatment-of-Mentally-Ill-Persons-in-the-Criminal-Justice-System.pdf
11. Harki, G. A. (2019, May 2). *Horrific Deaths, Brutal Treatment: Mental Illness in America's Jails | Prison Legal News.* Prison Legal News. https://www.prisonlegalnews.org/news/2019/may/2/horrific-deaths-brutal-treatment-mental-illness-americas-jails/
12. *Nearly a Fifth of State and Federal Prisons had at Least One Suicide in 2019.* (2021, October 7). Office of Justice Programs. https://www.ojp.gov/sites/g/files/xyckuh241/files/archives/pressreleases/2021/nearly-fifth-state-and-federal-prisons-had-least-one-suicide-2019
13. Harki, G. A. (2019, May 2). *Horrific Deaths, Brutal Treatment: Mental Illness in America's Jails | Prison Legal News.* Prison Legal News. https://www.prisonlegalnews.org/news/2019/may/2/horrific-deaths-brutal-treatment-mental-illness-americas-jails/.
14. *Ibid.*
15. Novick, L. (Director). (2019). *College Behind Bars.* Skiff Mountain Films.
16. *BOP: Work Programs.* (n.d.). Federal Bureau of Prisons. https://www.bop.gov/inmates/custody_and_care/work_programs.jsp#:%7E:text=Federal%20Bureau%20of%20Prisons&text=Sentenced%20inmates%20are%20required%20to,hour%20for%20these%20work%20assignments
17. *Prison Life—1865 to 1900 - Ancestry Insights.* (n.d.). Ancestry.Com. https://www.ancestry.com/historicalinsights/prison-life-united-states-after-civil-war
18. Schlaht, L. (2021, September 23). *History on Repeat: The Sordid Reality of Prison Abuse in the U.S.* The Legal Examiner. https://www.legalexaminer.com/legal/inmate-abuse/history-on-repeat-the-sordid-reality-of-prison-abuse-in-the-u-s/

19. Nearly a Fifth of State and Federal Prisons had at Least One Suicide in 2019. (2021, October 7). Office of Justice Programs. https://www.ojp.gov/sites/g/files/xyckuh241/files/archives/pressreleases/2021/nearly-fifth-state-and-federal-prisonshad-least-one-suicide-2019

20. Harki, G. A. (2019, May 2). Horrific Deaths, Brutal Treatment: Mental Illness in America's Jails | Prison Legal News. Prison Legal News. https://www.prisonlegalnews.org/news/2019/may/2/horrific-deaths-brutal-treatment-mental-illness-americas-jails/.

21. *Prison Conditions*. (2021, March 10). Equal Justice Initiative. https://eji.org/issues/prison-conditions/

22. The Sentencing Project. (2018, December). *The Facts of Life Sentences*. https://www.sentencingproject.org/wp-content/uploads/2018/12/Facts-of-Life.pdf

23. Rovner, J. (2023, April 7). *Juvenile Life Without Parole: An Overview*. The Sentencing Project. https://www.sentencingproject.org/policy-brief/juvenile-life-without-parole-an-overview/

AFTER PRISON

1. Novick, L. (Director). (2019). *College Behind Bars*. Skiff Mountain Films.
2. *Ibid.*
3. *Ibid.*
4. Cantürk, M., Faraji, H., & Tezcan, A. (2021). The relationship between childhood traumas and crime in male prisoners. *Anatolian Journal of Psychiatry*, 22, 1–5. https://doi.org/10.5455/apd.111825
5. Zoukis, C. (2023, June 25). *Prison education reduces recidivism*. Law Offices of Grant Smaldone. https://federalcriminaldefenseattorney.com/prison-education-facts/prison-education-reduces-recidivism/
6. *Life after Prison Success Stories - Stand together*. (2023, October 11). Stand Together. https://standtogether.org/news/6-stories-of-transformation-from-prisoner-to-professional/

IMAGES

Barbed wire image designed using images from: Freepik.com.

www.ingramcontent.com/pod-product-compliance
Lightning Source LLC
Chambersburg PA
CBHW070532160426
43199CB00014B/2248